Finding Your Way Through Therapy: A Navigation Tool for Therapists and Clients

© 2020 Steve Bisson, LMHC

Published by Steve Bisson LMHC

In Collaboration With Straight to the Point Publishing

Editor: Ashley Furtado

Book cover and design: Altered Lines

D1226123

Table of Contents

To my girls, Catherine and Christina. I will always love you.

To my friend who inspired my work, Avi. RIP

Prologue

At 12 years old, I lost my best friend in a house fire.

I was in shock from the event, and did not know who to turn to in order to talk about this pain I was feeling. It didn't help that this happened during the era where it was believed that 'real men' and 'big boys' didn't cry. So I buried it. By the following year, I could not bear to go to football. The reason; my best friend was on my team for 4 years. I blocked for him, he was the running back, I was an offensive lineman. My life had changed, on and off the field. I started shutting down all activities, and while I made new friends, they didn't even know about my secret. I did not want to fall apart in front of them. To this day, these friends, who are now friendships of 30+ years, are still surprised that I never talked about it then. Truthfully, I did my best to block it out. I'm not sure I wanted to remember him.

I think that event is partly why, when I was 16 or so, I realized that I wanted to be a therapist. My 'aha' moment is two-fold: first, what better way is there to earn a living than by sitting down and listening to other people's problems? While I was not the best listener, I knew I would be able to do this job due to the advice my mother gave me. I mean, I was told I talked too much anyway, maybe learning to quiet down enough to listen to others may be a good thing. All I knew was that I was looking forward to sitting down, listening to people's problems, and telling them how to solve it (by the way, it was not the only reason, but give me a break! I was 16). I will always remember that my mom had given me the book "Feeling Good: The New Mood Therapy" by David Burns (1) one summer and I devoured it. This therapist stuff seemed to be a breeze with CBT (Cognitive Behavioral Therapy) and cognitive distortions! It had even helped me with my issues. Even today, I dust off the book occasionally and use it whenever I need to utilize it.

Getting into this field, on the other hand, meant clawing my way in. I had trouble getting into a bachelor level program in Quebec, and then battled to get into a job in psychology out of college. I also struggled to get into a master's program. I had to leave my home city (Montréal), province (Québec), and country (Canada) and get a job in the United States of America. I had decided to get my masters here, as it was easier to get into a superb program. I was working 40+ hours a week (work permit obligation) and doing an internship of 15 hours a week for a year, which was exhausting. That's just the tip of the iceberg, do not forget attending classes, homework, and dating!

I knew social service jobs were not exactly a gateway to becoming a millionaire (never was my intention but come on, I must live) but I did not realize how poorly masters level clinicians and therapists were paid. While I will never cry poverty, it is true that mental health and social work are two of the worst paid master's level jobs out there (Mental health is the second worse, social workers are seventh worse) (2). And the pressure that we have with everyone's problems, mandated reporting, as well as the difficulty of leaving the work *at* work can easily consume you. How can you not think of someone's issues/trauma, or breakthroughs when you get home?

It is a tough job, and through my work on a crisis team, outpatient counseling with all socio-economic, gender, race, and/or religious backgrounds, collaborations with law enforcement on different levels, in schools, and literally therapy online, I have had many moments of doubt. Why am I doing this? Is it worth it? I lost so many clients to different medical ailments (screw cancer), to homicide, to suicide, to overdoses, and everything else. I lost clients who stopped seeing me because they did not like what I said or misunderstood me. It is so easy to turn anger towards myself on these issues and/or them. Maybe I am just not that good enough? Having self-doubt when you do something you love is so easy.

But then, I realized what I knew a long time ago: I love most of it. I keep on reminding myself of what brought me to this work, what I love about it, and how rewarding emotionally it is to help others through some very dark times. I forget sometimes, like most of us, the value of my connectedness with others. Connectedness is what makes us a better person, a better group of people, a better community, and to hopefully create a better world.. We are all interconnected. I can connect with individuals one person at a time…and they come back. How lucky is that?

I also know that people on their deathbed do not talk about how much money they made, how that financial deal brought joy to others, or who they possibly screwed over to get it. What do they talk about the most? "So much wasted time", as David Cassidy once said (3). Most wish they spent more time connecting with others. I also know that with the individuals I see who work in the business world who tell me how lucky I am to do my job, that I help others, and that my job is rewarding for that. While a bigger salary is always welcomed, I also realize that I go to bed every night knowing that I may have had an impact on others in a positive way. When I hear in therapy "I heard your words in my head" ,"I could sense what you would say" or "what would Steve say about this?". Those are priceless. One of my favorite quotes from one of my clients is: "You and your fucking tools, I use them now."

The spiritual journey that work brings me on a regular basis is awesome. While I still have my doubts (and, by the way, all therapists, counselors, and clinicians should have a healthy dose of doubt), I also know that there are several people who were my clients that are out there who carry around ideas, suggestions, and tools that I provided for them. These instruments make an impact in their lives in a positive way and hopefully, to our world. Wherever you sit on the spiritual journey of your life, this must be a human goal. I like the fact that my humanity has shown through my work and it has such an influence on my day to day work with others.

So why write this book? Because I know that I have supervised and/or mentored many other clinicians who I consider successful, who have told me that my support has had a positive impact on them. My clients have told me my unique ways of conducting therapy has been helpful and very comforting. It is also what brings them back every session. I also know that many who struggle with finding therapists that feel like a good fit need some direction on how it works.

Others have asked me, how exactly do I do this type of work, my way? Finally, I wanted to do my best to help others be better at their work, at this journey called life. If you find one or two tidbits that are helpful in this book, I feel it was worthwhile. This book only endorses my type of counseling and I want to make sure that anyone reading this can find their own style, get the info they need, and dismiss what they wish. Clients may need a different style for therapy, and it's important to remember that it is OK for them to ask for what they need. This book is just my own meandering thoughts.

I do not do anything special, I just try to be me as ethically, professionally, and authentically as humanly possible.

Who should read this book?

For Therapists:

One of the greatest compliments I have ever had from my colleagues is how they feel that I have the ability to really connect with clients. I also know that I respond to a specific clientele, which is another compliment that I have received from my supervisors, colleagues, and clients themselves. This is something that needs to be done for a great therapeutic relationship. While the techniques and ideas that I share here are good ways to bridge the gap with our clients, it is not, by any means an exhaustive list.

The techniques I discuss here are an excellent starting point. These are meant to be taken as my own thoughts on what works. Some are validated in an empirical way, some are my own discoveries along the way, and some are just ideas. One of the things that I do not want anyone to do is use this book as a "This is the only way" mentality. I offer these suggestions as ideas, as a best practice that have worked out for me in the last 20 years of my work in this field.

I have supervised many individuals in various settings, such as in a community mental setting, criminal/community justice settings, private practice, and even residential settings. What I write here is a general list of advice for what works for me. I do believe an honest, joining, personal approach is probably the best way in all those settings. Being yourself was taught to me at an early point in my career, from a client, as well as my supervisor at my internship. It is what continues to carry me to this day. The best and most notable empirical evidence that has been proven over the years regarding which technique works (CBT, DBT, ABA, EMDR, RET, Gestalt, ABC, XYZ, etc.) is the therapeutic alliance.(4)

Connecting cannot be taught in a book (or any book for that matter). Ultimately, you may find your own strategies (please send them my way), but the following chapters are techniques that have been successful for me. I think that lesson came from working 13 years on a crisis team. The greatest gift from my work there is that I learned how to work with many different people, from all walks of life. In an emergency room, you can evaluate kids as young as three or four and meet older individuals who are in their 80s and 90s.

You also see people at their worse. It is a very vulnerable place to be in and sometimes, the right words, referral, and treatment will help them to think differently. Your ability to connect with them is key. I really feel that this has brought me to where I am at this point in my career and where my eclectic style has become helpful for diverse populations. Working on crisis teams has helped me adapt to where the individual is at and not take any criticism personally. If you meet someone where they are, and you do not personalize any negative feedback, you can do well in multiple settings. It is personal but it is not: the balance of understanding where it is will hopefully be clearer by the end of the book. This is especially important in our work.

Finally, while my boundaries seem to be fluid, and they are, there are also certain things you need to clear up in order to make the limitations noticeably clear. I talk about how to reach me, attendance, as well the regular disclosures for HIPAA (never forget to say them out loud to a client, even though they 'know' them). I also encourage you to add a little quirk about yourself. I always share that my ability to remember names is not particularly the greatest. That way, they know something about me but also do not personalize if I forget a name they may have mentioned.

In the last chapter of the book, I discuss how to demystify therapy and make sure that therapists do not fall in certain traps. We tend to overlook many things as therapists, and I have done it myself. It is a great reminder for me when I look at some of these points, and I would like to think that it would be helpful to others.

Hopefully, some of the techniques discussed in this book will help therapists get an idea as to how to meet these individuals, in order to gauge where they are at when they decide to seek counseling.

For Clients:

I would encourage clients to read the paragraphs above, as it is as much about them as it is for therapists.

Many of my clients have said that I have had a unique style. One of the other compliments that I like to receive is when clients tell me that they have never had therapy quite like this before. They feel that this is beneficial. I also think that the nonjudgmental stance is one thing, but learning to get there is exceedingly difficult, both for the client and the therapist.

My clients have also told me that they do not feel that I am just sitting there passively. Being able to find an active listener with the ability to meet them where they are is key for a healthy therapeutic relationship. I believe that all they want is to be accepted in their discussion. Trying to force change or certain discussions can be the most detrimental thing a therapist can do.

If you are a client, I always discuss their options. I am not a therapist for everyone, and I recognize that. I think that being able to recognize your limitations and not being able to connect with everyone is key. Not all therapists are made for all clients and making sure that you can have that conversation is especially important. As a client, this book can clarify how to ask for what you need.

Reading about how I conduct my therapy may be beneficial for clients for several reasons: I encourage asking questions and really reaching out for a therapist that will be a good fit for you. I do not think that we should ever settle as clients. We need to figure out what the therapist is bringing us and if we are still getting what we need from them throughout the therapeutic relationship.

Being in therapy myself has helped shape my therapeutic relationships with my clients. Being able to see how it feels, to be sitting in the other chair so to speak, clearly has shown me how it can be very exposing and difficult to do. I also learn all the right questions to ask my therapist to make sure that I get what I want out of it. Hopefully, this shows in my style with my clients and that you get what you need from your therapist when you meet with them.

I am hoping that this book also helps you look at what you want out of therapy. My style is one of many and while I do believe that I match up well with the clients that I do have, my style is not unique nor is it the only one. The therapeutic relationship is one of the most unique ones in the medical field and as a client, you need to be able to look for a good match, not just for one who is available Thursdays at 3pm.

Chapter 1: Being Real

Keywords: Authentic, Choice, Conditionals, Confidence, Connectedness, Dirty Words, Genuine, Human, Professional, Regrets, Self-Talk, Simple, Yourself

The new millennium has brought us a slew of "reality" shows, which allegedly shows us what happens to everyday people, privileged people, celebrities, or people put in competition with each other. They display raw emotions, show how we react to different things and make the participants feel relatable, as if these events would have you react similarly if the same thing happened to you. Sometimes, it even makes you think of how you would react with the situation, and if the reality star would do the same thing.

As some know by now, many of those shows are scripted partly or even totally, down to the "season" finale. While the script usually gives the 'character' general lines, it is interesting to see how they react. It is important to note that life is sometimes stranger than fiction. These shows are/were believed to be a true display of what happens to individuals and their reaction to what we perceive as life. It can be validating, fulfilling or heartbreaking, depending on what happens in those situations.

Some have felt it was a bad thing to add this type of casting to TV. It was and continues to be a double-edged sword. It can help us relate to others who are showcased on those shows, make us feel like we are not the only ones with those problems, as well as show celebrities in vulnerable states, most importantly as humans. But it also made some feel small, boring, uninteresting, and frankly, that our lives are not as cool. It negates our own lives in very strange ways. Comparisons happen frequently when watching these shows.

From my perspective, I applaud the real emotions, the real issues, and the real reactions of some people finding it difficult to watch embarrassing situations. The important word to me is *real*. Real has become difficult to find in many situations, not only in reality TV but in general, in one on one discussions, and in our daily lives, and social media. Most reactions, pictures, and emotions displayed on social media are measured and mostly free of authenticity. It is thought that it takes, on average, 7 selfies before a person posts it.(5) When you learn about what really goes on, it can be seen as stranger than an episode of *Black Mirror*.

When you communicate with individuals, you must learn to display authentic, genuine emotions.

While it is important to be mindful of your client's perception, it is sometimes the calculated reactions that push them away. Clients are savvy about our authenticity and our realistic reactions. This is true of clients with trauma issues and clients who have been in the mental health system for a long time. When we communicate as therapists, we need to realize that clients can see right through any type of bogus reaction.

When we think authenticity, we mean that our reaction is real. Be surprised when you need to, be sad when you need to be, and show your client that your reactions are genuine. Being able to have reactions that show that you are listening and that the information they are providing can elicit a reaction can normalize their own feelings. If you sit across from your client looking identical to a statue, this can be perceived as coldness, and not something that will make a client feel validated. I encourage clients to find a good match on the subject.

We also must understand that genuine emotions are sometimes difficult to stomach for ourselves. It is a delicate balancing act to realize that sometimes our authentic reaction (for example, a traumatic event being described in detail) may force us to take a neutral stance so that the client knows we can take the information. A genuine expression of our perception may be more important after the fact. Using sentences like "I can only imagine" and "That is tough to hear, I can only imagine what it is to live it" are also especially important.

Another important point: while we are professionals, we are also humans. Most clients do not want to see a robot reaction, they want to see the human in you. While I think it is important to have a few sentences that you like to use that are available, saying things differently each time may show more authenticity. It also has been an observation in my counseling experience that the words we use may not always be understood, so being able to say the same thing differently helps the client understand and also avoids the embarrassment of asking what we meant. If you are going to say something, be able to explain it at least three different ways.

Therapists are taught through our schooling and internships that we "always" need to be nice and non-reactive. While it is appropriate in certain situations, I sincerely believe that the bulk of my clients have been relieved for my real reactions to their stories. Displaying shock to a horrible event will show that you join them in their struggles. I have rarely found a client who felt I could not handle it when I displayed real reactions to these situations. It comes back to the humanity piece I just discussed, which is key.

I also believe that this shows your ability to be yourself in your relationship with them. Being yourself, to me, is the cornerstone of your therapeutic relationship. Clients can relate to that and even feel that therapeutic connection they have sought for so long. They do want you to be realistic with them. Some clients have been in therapy with other therapists and they bring that baggage with them. They also have sensed the difference between authentic and real versus a rehearsed response.

One of the best things to do in therapy is to remain very realistic about what is going and realize change can be difficult. I will give credit to one of my best friends who once told me that she feels she is both not positive and not negative, she is a realist. I use that statement on a regular basis when people are too negative or positive and have trouble meeting in the middle. Being in the middle shows a good balance and avoids all or nothing thinking. In addition, realistic expectations can avoid the catastrophizing or over positivity. When you think of the individuals we see with the issues they face, they just don't want to be told to "Turn that frown upside down". Positive Psychology has validity, but it has also shown some limits with certain clients, so please make sure that above all, you are able to match your client. Toxic Positivity does exist.

Let them know it's tough to be this way, show some emotionality about what is being said, and do not overthink. Be real. I think that, as therapists, we are trained to be professional and that is a great thing (6). Let me be clear: I do not necessarily advocate for you to join clients in their sadness at every moment, as this will be detrimental in the long run. But show some emotional connection. I like to remind my clients that I am both. One of my favorite things to do is to let my clients know that as a therapist I will say "blank", but as a human, I believe "blank." While they want someone who is professional, they want a real response, not something that feels rehearsed and insincere.

As therapists, we are after all, human. I like to reiterate this fact. After some of my past work that made me lose my sense of humanity and cost me not only professional points and issues with my clients, it also cost me a lot on a personal level, something that I am no longer willing to sacrifice. I think of this time of my career a lot, as I grew leaps in bounds in many ways, but lost my connectedness, which includes my ability to relate to my clients in the name of doing something for my work. I must be me to feel my best at home and at work.

This was a price that I had to pay to be real. Yes, it was the real me. The hardened, do not care about others, 'they are not clients but suspects', *me*. It is something that I have regretted previously in my life and I did say that to some people. At this moment, however, I no longer regret it. At this moment, I realize that it made me a better person and woke me up. It was a price to pay but I can not blame others for that, I can only blame myself and my choices. I like to paraphrase a Quebec singer, who was very successful at one time but had to be lobotomized (which means they cut into her brain's corpus callosum, in the name of curing it for mental health reasons) before she regained some success before dying. One of her last interviews, she was asked "Do you have any regrets?" She paused and then said: "But I have no regrets. My greatest love affair has always been with show business. It's a tremendous life! You get to meet all kinds of people, to understand life. And I think you get to become very human, very tolerant" (7).

I really think that this is a good life lesson for all of us. We need to realize that regrets are something that we cannot control. It is the past. Nothing we can do about it. But can we learn from it today so that we do not make those mistakes again in the future? Of course, even if we have no control of the future and I understand that. But we do control ourselves today and how we process the information. I think it is so easy for us to remove ourselves from the past. But it happened. It was there, and it was probably something we don't wish to relive, but we still must acknowledge it happened and make peace with it.. Why worry about the past? Let us learn from these events and go forward.

Which brings me to the fear of the future. Being real means you remain in the present. Most of us know the saying: "the past is done, we cannot change it, the future hasn't happened, so we cannot control it, all we have is the present." You don't worry about the future because it has not happened. Staying here also means not using the conditionals that can be of hindrance. I have a sign in my office that a great friend of mine made for me. It is a take on the great George Carlin's seven dirty words (8). Mine are as follows:

If

But

Try

Should

Could

Would

Probably.

Why are these swear words for me? Because they are conditional. I want people to do things, I do not want them to do things conditionally.

Using those words limits you and your ability to get things done. I have never been a stickler for language, English is my second language, but one thing I have learned over the years is that the way we use language to talk about ourselves, as well as others really impact our lives. I have seen it countless times and how these things do make a difference. Whether it is the conditional language I am talking about here, or the self-talk that we use, it all impacts how we deal with stuff and how this will bring us to complete tasks or even believe in our abilities. It is key to our own self-esteem and our ability to be able to be more confident in our work.

Speaking of which, I like to remind my clients that your self-doubt is something that others can read off of you. Learning to exude confidence is key. And the language plays a factor. I think that if we only saw how our self-doubt and negative self-talk kills most of the opportunities we can get, we'd be horrified at ourselves. It is important to "fake it until you make it" which seems so counterintuitive to what this chapter is all about. When all else fails, learning to talk about it in a confident way may change the perception of others. Being confident, not arrogant, will change how you communicate and make you appear more real and more natural. No one will doubt your words if you say with confidence "Aw, people can come up with statistics to prove anything Kent, 14% of people know that ("The Simpsons" reference)"(9). At the end of the day, your realness will come through.

To be real means so many things but learning to trust yourself, trust your words, live in the moment, and all while being realistic will carry you as a therapist and as a person in general.

Chapter 2: Honesty is Hardly Ever Heard

Keywords: Acceptance, CBT, Constructive, Cruelty, Disagreements, Empathy, Ethics, Instincts, People Pleasing, Social Media, Tactful

I was told as a child that honesty is the best policy.

It is one way to get out of trouble, receive support from loved ones when something went wrong, and even obtain some praise at times. Honesty was something valued and supported by others. TV shows would praise it, my teachers would say it, my neighbors would show it, and police officers would value it. The Catholic church was particularly great at imposing it. This recovering Catholic knows about this a little too well. I grew up Catholic and I remember having to go to confession daily for my sins. Although my parents never forced me, it did reinforce the fact that we lie everyday. Or so we were told.

As I grew older, I noticed the people around me started to make sure that I was not 'always' honest. Although it was subtle, it was mostly eye glances that were either long, or very angry expressions that I learned to interpret quickly. It was a way to let me know that not all truths needed to be told. If I said something that wasn't 'sugarcoated' to people, I would defend myself by saying that it was the truth ("the whole truth, and nothing but the truth"). I felt like this was a life lesson I had finally nailed; how come I wasn't getting the credit I thought I deserved? I was then informed that truths do not always need to be told. You must be careful and remember not to talk about certain subjects to certain people. It's just like when you go on a first date, and all your friends advise you to definitely not talk about religion, politics, among other controversial topics. You come to a point in your life where you think, "Wait a minute! You imposed this on me for years and suddenly it is wrong? How can that be?"

As a result, I became the nice guy. What I mean by that is I started telling people what they wanted to hear, instead of what was the truth. It was the right thing to do, correct? Remember, do not be honest if it is going to hurt. Which also led me to not telling everyone the truth about what I considered flaws about me. I wasn't lying, right? I was just being nice and trying to protect others. I have now discovered that I was also protecting one important person at the time, myself. That is what I had to do to protect others from the truths about themselves, so what is good for them should be good for me, right?

While all of us do not have the exact same stories, I do believe our stories can be so similar that they almost touch. It might feel that we were all taught to be truthful, but not all the time, after all if you lie to protect others, that makes it okay. No wonder we never know when to be truthful about anything! We learn to lie not only about ourselves to others, but also to ourselves about us. It's no wonder we are so confused as humans since we are constantly given mixed messages about what is right and wrong. But do not lie to protect yourself no matter what, especially as a teenager. When it comes to the elderly, be kind to them. No matter what, telling your grandmother her purple hair looks great is kindness, not lying! And your boss, unless they ask for an honest answer, then *definitely* lie. For a friend, well, judge their mood and go from there.

We want to protect ourselves on a regular basis about what others think about us, as well as what we think of others. I have learned that for some people keeping themselves safe from their own judgement and others means lying to themselves. It is something that some psychoanalysts would possibly call denial(10). After all, it is not just a river in Egypt! It is the phenomenon where we block external events from awareness. It may be because the truth can be too much to handle, so we just block it from our own awareness. It appears to be a good way to keep ourselves safe from a situation or other phenomenon. It is not a long-term effective tool but may be part of a shorter-term goal. While defense mechanisms have a bad reputation, there is a reason why we developed them.

As for cognitive behavioral therapists, they would call that cognitive dissonance (11). This occurs when a person who experiences inconsistency tends to become psychologically uncomfortable, they are then motivated to try to reduce the cognitive dissonance from occurring. This typically results in them actively avoiding situations and information that are likely to increase the psychological discomfort. In many ways, this is similar to how we avoid being honest with others, in order for us not to feel 'awkward' or 'uncomfortable' we simply sugarcoat what we have to say or stay silent all together. We change and adjust our own thoughts to fit the "socially accepted" response to what is in front of us. If we are able to convince ourselves that we are doing this for the greater good of avoiding conflict, we will distort our reality to make it work the way we want, hence lying to ourselves.

The Rogerians, on the other hand, would let the dishonesty happen and regard it as something a client will eventually catch on and address(12). It is not a bad thing that the client is doing it. It is something they do to make themselves understand things better. A safety net if you will. A Rogerian will not confront the lie but continue to emphasize how it is important to believe what we say. We do not want to tell the client they may be lying, as this would create an issue with the unconditional positive regard we must have for the client. If we let the client sit on the feeling through thought reflection and unconditional positive regard, it will eventually work itself out.

Truth is great, truth is hard, truth is powerful. Truth is good when used properly. Truth is difficult to do at first but eventually, we can make it easier on ourselves, as well as others by doing it regularly. Truth is the most powerful tool you will ever have in your life. With truth, who needs to use all that energy to remember what they said and in which context, as well as to whom? Just like anything else, being truthful is neither good nor bad, it is what you do with it that is key. The message of truth is our responsibility, how others receive it, and how you do not get to tell them how to feel about it. After all, it is their truth and their interpretation. How can that be wrong? You need to remember your responsibility when transmitting the truths to others.

We need to be truthful to ourselves first if we ever want to succeed. Being able to speak to ourselves in an honest way is probably the best gift you can ever give yourself in the long run. It is where it all starts. We can accomplish that by knowing our strengths and weaknesses. We have both, so let us acknowledge them. I like to think of one of my favorite authors, the late Debbie Ford, who talked about how we are everything, and accepting these truths can be the key for us to evolve to the best of our abilities(13). Debbie talks about not compulsively running from one end to another. When you embrace who you are, you no longer have to live in fear. Recognizing that we are both selfish and selfless is important, as this will not make us avoid one or the other. When we realize this, we can truly be proud of who we are.

Let me give you an example of what she is talking about. As a therapist, and likewise to marriage vows, I think with the mentality of "for better or for worse." I sometimes extend my sessions at my clients' requests or needs, depending on the circumstances. In that way, I am selfless. I even take texts and emails from my clients and spend time reading them off hours. However, I would not do it if I were working for free all the time (this is where selfishness comes into play). At the end of the day, I get paid to do my job. While I love the work I do, earning a paycheck is an essential reason why we have jobs.

How does this relate to honesty? If you look at one of the most common issues in truth telling, being a people pleaser, there is appeal in that you seem to get along with others...until you disagree. How can you be both? The people pleaser tends to avoid conflicts and does not feel they can do that by disagreeing. The people pleaser also wants to be liked, but they often equate that to no conflict or disagreement with anyone. It is a good feeling to "get along" always with others. It makes you feel like a good person: a person who does good, and who has a good knack of getting along with others no matter what. However, that is seemingly impossible when you believe in the truth. Truth is sometimes a creator of conflict but in conflict, there is a possibility of growth.

Truth, however, does not have to hurt. We often equate the truth with a hurtful state. I think that we need to accept that the truth can be unpleasant and sometimes downright unkind. Regardless if you always see it in that negative light, it will remain negative for a long time. Truth can be gentle in nature if done the right way. Truth, in fact, can blossom relationships by encouraging discussion and open-mindedness. Being able to have conflict with others without seeing it as an end all that be all will also make the relationship grow, and even makes the relationship stronger than it was before. The strongest bonds I have with friends are the ones who don't say things just to please me.

If you are honest with yourself, you will know that disagreements can be constructive, helpful, as well as a way of growing. I also believe that honesty, when said appropriately, can be positively received and will further your self-appreciation and self-growth. People pleasing can also come via gentle honesty. I think if we learn how to do it in a constructive, nonaggressive/judgmental way, lots of people can be very open to talking about some of the more difficult subjects. I also believe that, when done with people who are comfortable with you in addition to the setting, many thoughts can come out honestly, with lots of room for great feedback and constructive support.

One of my favorite broadcasters, Howard Stern, has revolutionized radio. I will talk about him, his techniques, and his style of interview a few times in this book, as he is a masterful interviewer. He is able to make his guests feel so comfortable that they forget about who is in the room, the cameras around them, and the millions listening around the world(13). He is very controversial, but to me, he has dialed down his persona in the last few years to have a more universal appeal. as well as to understand what he is trying to accomplish by saying certain things. Howard has matured in one of the best interviewers on the radio, if not the best. He has a way with words, and he has been to therapy himself for several years. The fact that he has been so open about his therapy has helped break stigma and barriers with his audience about therapy, as well as created an open dialogue regarding its benefits.

You can fixate on what you want about him. He has been known as a "shock jock", a controversial figure who has gotten many interviewees in trouble for saying things in the heat of the moment. As a therapist, there are few things that strike me as great processes to emulate. One of the things he mentions in his movie "Private Parts", as well as in his broadcasts, is that he blurts things out as he feels them. It is something that he is known for and has caused him to get in trouble with others at times. Blurting out things can be risky and can cause many issues, He does not apologize for his style and what he does is extremely hard to replicate (see numerous jocks who tried to emulate him but never could capture that magic). How can that be translated to counseling sessions?

Most of us, especially therapists, overthink what we are going to say during a conversation. It is in our ethical duty and job responsibility to make sure we say things that are appropriate and may not provoke or upset our clients. We sometimes do not trust our instinct. We have ideas that pop out in our mind, but they seem farfetched. Why would I say something that could be out of the blue? Can I really be sure my client is ready for this statement or question? Yet, it is essential, and it is a gift. Call it intuition, call it psychic abilities, but anyway you want to call it, there is a reason it comes up in your head. Say it and I would present it as "let me tell you what popped in my head." Why should we use this technique?

You never want to be wrong, so most of us will try to make sense, logically, of what we are going to say. In doing so, we lose the first instinctual thought by making a "logical" statement to the person we are talking to. It dilutes our message and it sometimes makes us lose the essence of what we are truly trying to say. We overcomplicate things that can be said honestly and more directly. It is when we speak honestly, from the original instinct, that you can make real progress with someone. Howard Stern is known for making people talk this way.

There is a song by a Quebec artist called Luc de la Rochelière, which has one of my favorite quotes: "Everybody wants to be loved by everyone but no one loves everyone (this is loosely translated)"(14). I have yet to meet a person that is loved by everyone, and I know most people do not love everyone. It is a fact of life, and it is something that is an all or nothing statement that needs to be moderated, which will help you see the middle ground. We are not loved by everyone, so logically if we try to people please, aren't we doomed to fail eventually? Let us be honest; we need to accept this truth to move forward in our lives. How many of us feel that this statement is relatable and makes sense?

I really believe our need for acceptance has taught us to bury the truth deep inside ourselves to feel accepted. Social media has been a prime example. While we might seem obsessed with social media, we are only obsessed with the socially acceptable posts, while avoiding the nastier parts of social media. It is imperative to get the dreaded likes, retweets, favorites, etc. which most social media users crave. There have been so many instances where people continue to do things to see how many likes they get. In fact, over 70% of individuals recheck their social media to see any commentary, likes, love or other acceptable feedback from others about their tweet, Instapic, status update, etc.(15). However, are we being honest with others when posting these statuses and pictures? More importantly, are we being honest with ourselves?

Social media has filled us with lies on many occasions, and studies have suggested that it can cause depression, anxiety, and lack of empathy(16). I think we also tend to react quickly instead of being thoughtful. We read these things or look at these pictures and we seek to react as it is the socially desirable thing to do, even when we disagree. When email first came out, people tended to react too quickly, and would end up replying too fast without thinking, with the belief they had to answer right away. Now, it is social media, and I am dreading the consequences from the creation/use of the dislike button. While it could be fun, it also may lead to bullying.

Which brings me to the current state of social media use. It has caused most individuals to be "honest" about their feelings, particularly as it pertains to their political views and who they do not like or who can be thrown on to their pages, with little to no room for disagreement or objection. We have become such bullies overall in these social media apps. Oh, you do not agree? You are almost (ok *most* of the time) defriended, blocked, or removed from your circle. You get a reaction that is equivalent to hate in some instances. While it is sometimes very frustrating when others cannot see your point of view, social media has used "honesty" to give permission to extremely negative comments about others.

I wonder if honesty can be a way to explore your own point of view. It could be used to see how you can explore the possibility that another point of view can be accurate, that might not be the same as what we personally believe. It has been quite clear in the past few years that we have been divisive in many Westernized cultures. That is done in the name of "truth", a truth that is visible to the one who is conveying the message. But what about being able to see the other side without agreeing? I use the words "I agree to disagree" in session on a regular basis. Not to please others, but instead to create space for disagreement.

Honesty is not used to hurt others. I think it is the biggest misconception about the truth. Truth can be conveyed without hurt, whether it is on social media or face to face with anyone you know. Truth is not meant to hurt, but it can have that side effect. Being able to see where it can hurt is helpful to convey the empathy and sympathy to the other person who could be hurt by what you say. You need to be able to use the honesty displayed to be more direct, especially when making sure it is something that can grow and prosper any type of relationship.

One of my inspirations in my quest to define honesty comes from actress Kristen Bell, from an interview she gave to a reporter which made its rounds in the therapeutic circles I frequent online. I have always loved her as a human and as Elsa's sister in another movie I like, *Frozen*. She has had genuine interviews on many shows, including on Howard Stern. She was talking about some of the things she learned from her therapist and he had a great thought in regard to honesty.

"Honesty without tact is cruelty" (17). This statement made me ponder a few things in regards to honesty in counseling. The first thing was that honesty is a lot trickier than I could ever imagine. It is a delicate balance of many things, including being truthful without hurting the other person's feelings. While on the surface this seems easy, think about it a little deeper. As a therapist, we sometimes are tempted to omit the truth to "protect" our clients. So how do we remain truthful, tactful, all while trying to protect our clients?

The answer is not easy, but I do believe that balance does exist. I think that we can have an honest reaction and be tactful about it. Saying things like, "I'm surprised" as well as expressing how it felt different to you as a therapist can be truthful, tactful and can help move the process along. Protecting our clients' feelings is not an option in my opinion but being able to spare a hurtful reaction is definitely recommended. It will come with time and experience, but our ability to be honest without destroying our clients is key. I know, easier said than done!

Honesty does have a place in all aspects of life, and we must accept this to move forward. If you are honest while measuring your words, this can be both liberating for you, as well as for the receiver. The honest point of view and how you communicate it is the responsibility of the person delivering the message, not the receiver. Receiving the truth can be difficult, but it does not always have to hurt.

Chapter 3: Winds of Change

Keywords: Addiction, Control, Desire, Difficulties, Expectations, Failures, Homeostasis, People Pleasing, Predictability, Realistic

Change is probably the surest thing in life but also one of the most difficult things to accept. We have all conveyed to someone at some point that we want to change or that we want *something* to change. But how many of us genuinely want to change while knowing how tough it can be?

It has been my experience that change is sought but is rarely easy to find by the individual seeking it. Yet, when you do offer the solution for it, you encounter tremendous resistance. This can be a difficult reality to accept for several reasons. The first reason is that it will force you to do something different. That is always harder than staying the same. As creatures of habit, we struggle with an easy change. Try, for example, to change hands when using utensils. Let me know how that works out for you. Observe someone who has an injury having to use the other hand or walk "normally" after having a temporary loss of the use of their dominant limbs. We look clumsy, we look awkward, and we look like we do not know what to do. I have also seen many say: "Is this worth even doing?" I believe that when we try to adopt change, we have the best intentions in the world, yet going through it, well, sucks.

If you really think about it , does anyone in these cases really want the change? Do they want to use the other limb, or do something in a new way? To adapt, they must do it, but it is not easy. To succeed, you must really want to do it. The hardest part of change is to find the motivation to change. Now let us think of a bad habit, such as an addiction. I like to define words, as this makes it easier to see the basis, I use in order to write about something. Addiction, according to the American Society of Addiction Medicine (ASAM) is: " a primary, chronic disease of brain reward, motivation, memory and related circuitry. Dysfunction in these circuits leads to characteristic biological, psychological, social, and spiritual manifestations."(18) I don't like to dilute the meaning of addiction but since it is one of the most common things people want to change, I wanted to use it here as an example.

Addictions are rarely something that a person wants to continue but, due to several factors, they continue that behavior. We can blame the person but ultimately, what is the true issue? Changing something you've become used to, that you are comfortable doing, will always be something that may be difficult to alter. While not everything is addiction, such as using your right hand, the analogy here can work when you think about how addiction develops and how the person wants to change it. There are no clients that I have ever met that told me, "Oh no, I wanted this addiction, get used to it, and then be told by many others I should stop it." Understand that wanting the change for people with addiction is not the lack of wanting, it is the lack of dealing with change. I will go on in detail about addiction in a later chapter.

When you really think about anything we do regularly, good or bad, isn't it an issue to move on from homeostasis? The body gets used to certain things and eventually starts expecting them. When it does not happen i.e. change, your body reacts on many levels. It does not want to do something different, after all, we are comfortable with no change. Staying the same brings predictability and regularity. I think that wanting the change for ourselves, no matter the other external pressures, is key. When you want to change to please others or frankly, to shut them up, does that type of change typically stick for anyone?

The key to change is wanting it for us and only us. Some will argue that change that is motivated by others can also work. In my experience, and in the many conversations with other therapists/counselors/clinicians, I have noted that if the desired change is not desired by the person, you will not sustain change. I am sure there is some research on the subject but if a person does not want change, there is little evidence that it will stick in the long-term. In my experience, change comes from our motivations, our own wants, and our abilities, not from the outside.

I am assuming that the next question will be: "But Steve, what can you do to change anything? I mean you are a therapist. You should know this like the back of your hand." One of the biggest misconceptions, despite my motto, is that therapists do not change people. Therapists, despite years of training and years of experience, have no control over the change of an individual, except when it comes to themselves. The point is that change is in the hands of the person requesting it. It is a great misconception that therapists have this uncanny ability to change someone.

What is true, is that therapists are the vessel that can bring change. While therapists cannot make change happen, we offer tools for anyone who has a desire to change. Hence my next point: having the desire to change. It is a misnomer that therapists have that ability. If you know therapists who bring change, there are two likely scenarios: one, they are lying or very unfamiliar of how the process works, or two, they have offered the right tools to the person at the right time, in the right way, and with great connection. They were able to offer the right balance of ideas, suggestions, and observations to bring along the desire of a client to move forward.

Change is something that requires a person to move forward with a plan that is mostly, if not all, their own. I like to remind both colleagues and clients that pushing others to change is not the best solution. Typically, people will change to please others or to make them stop talking. These are the wrong reasons to change. I have had many clients in my career wanting me to tell them what to do. I caution any therapist to tell a client what to do. The person requesting this may be well intended, but if they do anything the therapist says and it "doesn't work out", the therapist can be perceived as not able to help or that they give lousy advice. Therapists know this very well, because all therapists are just *so* stable and grounded (see the term facetious in a future chapter),Therapists have learned to discuss goals and paths to these goals, rather than telling the client exactly what to do.

What is a person going to learn if you tell them how to change, what to do, when to do it and how to manage it? I really feel like therapists are agents of change only if they let the client come up with solutions themselves, so that they can feel like they have the capacity to make the right decision, which will eventually lead them to the right change in their life. It is not the goal of therapists to keep people in counseling for the rest of their lives. It is to give their clients a different point of view without indicating the next move directly. Being good agents of change, therapists learn to hold back direct advice. This can be quite a challenge in a therapists' early career, as this is usually what brought them to the job in the first place, i.e. that they were able to give good advice and ideas to people.

Change is difficult and helping clients make those decisions versus making the decision for them is key. At the end of the day, the client will thank you. Most of my successful terminations are the ones where I let the client come up with the hard decisions by themselves, instead of telling them what I thought they should do. It is extremely important to make sure they can make healthy, informed decisions. But how do you know when to make more suggestions, rather than hold back with clients?

I think this is a good time to introduce the importance of the client's work. While I know I am hired by clients for a job, I also know that if I work harder than they do, change will not occur. What I mean by that, is that I like to see my clients show effort before I start working harder than them. They need to show what they have been doing to try to make changes in their lives, and how they have explored possibilities. Reaching out is a good first step of looking for solutions to what they want and to work towards this change but sometimes, it is more important to see what the client is willing to do to work on it.

What I like to explore is if the client is committed to the change. It is hard to find good techniques to measure that, but I have used a few tools as an indication. I start by looking at the attempts a person has made to reach the goals that they want to achieve. Past attempts can be a clear indication of where the person is at. Attempts are also very indicative of wanting to change, but maybe they are sometimes lacking certain qualities to do so. By reviewing what they have done in the past, you are able to observe a lot more of what needs to be changed to get to where the person wants to be. The past is not an indication of the future, but it is also an indication of failures that may have taken place in their attempts to change. I also want to note that failure has nothing to do with something negative, but an indication of where the person is standing now in their lives.

When we want to change certain parts of our lives, we must be able to see the worthy attempts of change that have occurred in the past. Furthermore, it is important to see if there are commonalities in regards to failure, especially if it was the cause of a certain situation. It is important to note that a person cannot want to change for other people as noted before. If the past indicates certain common threads, you need to explore those trends and see if these are currently occurring or not. It is important to note that if a person shows any indication of change because of only situations, or outside people/pressures, the possibility of permanent change tends to be significantly lower.

It is also important to see if the change is well thought out. This comes back to the motivation of the individual. While I am not a huge fan of the word motivation, looking at the possibilities of what brought them to the change process and what has pushed them currently is important. I find it interesting when people have never attempted to change, and then suddenly decide that they will reach out for the first time with a therapist. It becomes imperative for me, as a therapist, to make the person comfortable with where they are, as well as to show that change is possible, but it is also realistic to realize that change will be difficult.

One of the unrealistic expectations many clients have is that they believe they will be able to change in record time. What I like to remind my clients is that it took them years to look for and receive help to try to change. How can a therapist change that in several weeks? While change can be very quick, long-term change cannot be sustained if you do it too quickly. Quick change has value and it shows to the person who's doing the change that they can do it; however, quick change can also be a set up. When you change so quickly, you start expecting change to happen at a moment's notice throughout all the stages of change. Sustaining change is difficult and takes a lot of time. Reminding clients this when things are going well is key.

Therapists do not like to be the bearer of bad news. Well at least the therapists I know. Therapists do not go into this field to make people feel bad, but to make them feel better and sustain change. However, change takes time. The old adage is that it takes at least 21 days to sustain change (20). When people are changing quickly, I remind them of a few things, especially that change will take time to stick. While this may seem negative to some therapists and clients, I like to remind them that this is a realistic approach to change.

When people change very quickly, they typically get praise from others and start being enormously proud of themselves. This is all good stuff as positive reinforcement is key to help change be maintained. However, that praise goes away with time. I will talk about this further in the addiction chapter of this book. But let us do a quick intro to it right now. When you first sustain change, it is positive not only for you, but for the people around you to notice, there is a lot of praise and a lot of support that goes with it. After a while, however, people expect the change and do not praise it as much. The positive reinforcement slowly goes away and becomes an expectation. This is particularly difficult for those who use that external validation to feel better about themselves.

That is when I reiterate the point that change must be for yourself and not for others. Making changes for others is typically bad news. Making sure that they positively reinforce themselves on the change reminds themselves that they will not always skyrocket but that they will fluctuate. It is especially important to remember this when things are going well, not when things start going bad. If you wait that long, clients feel betrayed and frankly, I don't blame them. That is why my realistic approach to change has been well-received by most people. Not always in a moment, obviously. But in the long term, people appreciate the cautionary tales that I give them.

What about changing something that may be the source of the issue? I think it is so important to really find the root of the issue and start changing parts of it. If you can change something in the immediacy, that is a great thing. I obviously try to start there first. However, it is important to note that sometimes the changes that you make today may have other causes. If you can communicate to the client that the change of this behavior is excellent, there may be other moments where other things will rise up and they will make the change too. This keeps the client in a realistic view of what can happen in the future. Keeping them in the dark or feeling like they do not need to hear that for now is not beneficial for the therapeutic relationship and for a client.

What about if it is a combination of all this? In my experience, what I like to remind people is that there is never a singular solution for how a person wants to change. At the end of the day, there are so many things that can influence your behavior, attitude, or action when you want to change. Having a conversation in regards to the multiple sources of these things is key. I've yet to encounter a problem where a person only had one single source of stress because of it. To make change, it is important to address all these issues that require change, not just what is originally discussed in session. Letting the client come to those conclusions is tricky and putting it out there as a way to plant a seed is important.

You must be careful how you discuss changing with your clients. Being able to tell them that change will take time is important on several fronts. Therapy has been shown to be effective in the long term and not in a month or so (21). Explaining the reason for that is because the multiple layers that need to be addressed will keep the client engaged in counseling, instead of stopping where they're at. Encouraging the change is important but making sure they are also addressing the other issues surrounding change is sometimes more difficult to accept for most clients.

One final word in regards to change. You need to do the work before you make the change. While I do not want to go into deep detail on motivational interviewing, it is important to note that there is a contemplation and preparation period, where a person needs to do a lot of work in regards to what they need to do in order to help sustain the change. While everyone wants the change to take place, it is not as automatic as most people believe. It takes time to set up everything around it so that it sustains over a significant amount of time.

Change is not as easy as most believe. It needs to be done over time, and the process must be respected in order to get to where a person wants to be.

Chapter 4: A Beautiful Mind Needs to Be Nurtured

Keywords: Brain Anatomy, Change, Conditional Words, Neurology, Resistance, Thought Process, Trauma

The mind/body/spirit connection is another thing I emphasize in my practice and with most of my clients. While most people connect the work we do as 'brain stuff', there is a significant history of research that shows that this connection works well. Let me start by talking about the mind connection.

In the first couple of chapters, we discussed in depth how important it is to set up change, in order not to underestimate the importance of a good basis going forward. The first basis of this connection is the mind. While the brain gets lots of attention for different things, neuropsychology is still developing at a rapid pace(22). Many researchers have realized that the steps involved in neurological research have a significant impact on individuals. In other words, your biological world plays a huge factor in your ability to get to where you want to be. It will be important to pay attention to bring connection, as well as knowing how the brain is made. While I do not want to go into a biological discussion, I will provide a basis in this chapter.

Let us start with basic brain anatomy. The brain has been dissected in many ways, but most neuropsychological studies have shown that there are three important parts to distinguish(23). There is our cerebral cortex, which is the outer layer of our brain, where higher functioning thought processes and actions take place. Think about it as the part where you see all the wrinkles of your brain. The second part is the midbrain, which is the limbic-cortex system. This is where the fight or flight response lives, as well as where particularly important chemical releases take place. Many consider this part of the brain to be its most vital part, despite not being the higher functioning part(24). Finally, there is the hindbrain, which is where you will find your spinal cord, your cerebellum, and medulla oblongata. This is the part of the brain that you may have heard of in the movie "The Waterboy".

While I do not want to classify which part of the brain is the most important, it is important to note how our mind actually works before we start discussing a little bit more about the mind/body/spirit connection. When information is received in the body, it starts in the hindbrain, travels to the midbrain, and finally to the cerebral cortex in that order. This is significant because of the reaction that will be released. Just like Neanderthals, our basic core functions as humans are based on the reaction in the hindbrain and midbrain. When you react suddenly, it never reaches the cerebral cortex until much later. This is where we have everything controlled in her body that we consider unconscious. This includes breathing, heart rate, blood flow, etc.

When a person reacts to something fairly quickly, it typically stays in the hindbrain and midbrain. It is not a cerebral cortex reaction. That does not mean it never reaches the cerebral cortex, however it is a good rule of thumb when you see people reacting. Some might even call it our instincts. In my opinion, it is not important what you call it, but it is important to know that some of this is not really thought out. This makes perfect sense when we get to other parts of this discussion. I really feel that if we understood what makes us react, we would be much more controlled with our reactions, despite some of it not being under our control.

An important part of this is that the brain does not process emotions. Typically, we think of emotions as being on the cerebral cortex, or higher level. When people react, try to remember that it is not necessarily done in a very thoughtful way, but much more as an instinctual reaction from the mid-and hind brain (25). While not excusing those behaviors, it is important to note these things when we look at other people's reactions. I also like to remind people that our ability to hold back our initial reaction is key and may distinguish us from humans with higher functions versus what we would consider primitive animals.

Please understand that I am not judging these reactions. I am just saying that if you have the ability to see it in other people, you will note that it is not something that they have much control over. It is also important when you start processing your own reactions in regards to how you judge yourself. We typically judge ourselves very severely on our core reactions, but it is important to send a quick reminder to ourselves that this is not something under our control, and is probably a good way to not feel so negative about what we have done. Our judgment, again, is a higher brain function. It also gets clouded by other things, including morals and standards, all things that are typical in human beings that are not necessarily found in other animals.

I like to use the example of trauma in these situations. Our reactions typically reside in our fight or flight response which is the midbrain (26). It is not something that we necessarily have much control over, as it is an automatic response. Think about any type of trauma that you've heard of, including physical, emotional, and sexual trauma. When we hear it from other people or even ourselves, we start having these thoughts about what we should have done, could have done, if only things were different, etc. I will discuss these conditional statements and hindsight statements again later in this chapter. While trauma can reside anywhere in the brain, our reaction to trauma really is done at the mid or hindbrain.

Trauma Is a lot more common than we think. Don't worry, as I do not think that we are all trauma victims. I think that we all have different paths and different things have affected us differently. I have had many trauma discussions with people and they range from something that is highly publicized that most people know about to something very simple, such as a dead cat on the side of the road. I think that trauma is very personal and what has traumatized one person may not traumatize another. It is essential to realize that our brain is not traumatized by the same things as everyone else's. Trauma is personal but needs to be addressed.

I believe that a lot of different theories work on trauma, but I have done Eye Movement Desensitization and Reprocessing (EMDR), which has been specifically beneficial for people that have trauma that they cannot talk about or that causes significant distress to the point they cannot function (27). I have done tremendous work with this technique with first responders, military veterans, as well as people who have significant trauma that they have not been able to address otherwise. While some have stated that EMDR works in certain ways, the research does not indicate exactly how it works(28). When I am asked about this technique, I talk about how short-term memory is readily available and that traumatic events tend to stay trapped in your short-term memory. EMDR seems to take these traumas from the short term to the long term by engaging both hemispheres in the brain (29).

EMDR can be done by sound, by sight, or by touch. You use different instruments, such as an audio sound, which includes a movement of the fingers or paddles that vibrate to engage alternatively both sides of the brain. By doing so, as the theory goes, you can move a memory from short term to long term. EMDR works over several sessions, but it has been remarkably successful within weekly sessions for 8 to 10 weeks (30). The structures themselves are essential, but the most important part is that the client who is receiving it has full control and it is not a talk therapy situation. Clients have seen significant improvement per studies as well as my own observations in my few years doing it (31).

Trauma, of course, has other treatment modalities, including cognitive behavioral, as well as humanistic. Trauma is very difficult to treat as there are several guidelines to think about, which includes not inserting memories by suggesting ideas and making sure the client has enough resources and soothing techniques to get out of a tough spot when thinking of their trauma. Trauma work can be rewarding, but it is also lots of work to follow through. Most people who enter the profession want to help those who can't get past their past, but the work of healing trauma can be draining for both parties. Making sure that you normalize that for yourself, as well as your fellow practitioners, will make the long-term work on trauma more rewarding and realistic in expectations.

Lastly, I will discuss neuroscience. One of the most fascinating studies that I recently read is related to thoughts that individuals have in the day. These studies indicate that individuals have 12,000 to 60,000 thoughts daily (32). It is hard to wrap our head around this statistic, but ultimately, I tend to think that it is probably accurate. Think about it, while reading this chapter, you may have thought about the font, the noise around you, a thing you must remember, or any other thought that just shows up randomly. It is much more common than we think, and it has been difficult to display how important mindfulness and intention is key, but that spiritual discussion is offered elsewhere in this book.

My current theory on this subject is as follows: our initial thought that enters our brain is neutral, whether it is an observation, a thought, or idea. It has no value in itself. And I mean that in a baseline. But our interpretation takes over and that is where we attach the value. Is the value positive or negative? Depends on what emotions it creates in you. And learning to control how this emotion is interpreted is key. It may be positive initially but depending what channel you take it down, it can be negative. I also believe our own self beliefs play a factor in this process .

Knowing our tendencies in our brain is key. One of my main tenets of my work with my clients is to discuss conditional thought processes. This means that we do use words that seem to be a way to give ourselves an excuse to not complete things. It is important in life that we are able to look at ourselves in a more realistic fashion, especially when we have to be careful that we don't give ourselves a limiting self-talk, as well as saying it to others. While I've never been a huge proponent of words being a way to keep ourselves from completing things, I can see in some ways how our own thought processes, as well as how we use words, can be used as a way to avoid completing tasks.

I spoke earlier of my seven dirty words in my office, which is obviously a take on the late great George Carlin's work. I know that some of my clients have found this useful. I know some other clients are sick of me pointing at the sign. But I know one thing for sure is that they do remember it on a regular basis. Now let us look at these words and see why we should avoid these words, not just all the time, but on a regular basis.

To me, these conditions set you up to not complete a task. Let us use 'but' for example. I find that this is a word used on a regular basis by my clients when I make them uncomfortable about completing or doing something. If I give them a good example of things to do, I get the dreaded "yeah, *but.*" (For the record, "yeah but" is not a word). To me this is resistance. While resistance is not something that I'm opposed to, as resistance is part of the dialogue you can create to actually grow with your client, it is important to note that resistance also gives us a reason not to do it. One of the things that therapists struggle with is to challenge our clients, because we are sometimes afraid of the reaction or if we might lose them. At the end of the day, challenging those thoughts is important for many reasons.

As I discuss in the change chapter, "yeah but" prevents change. It is important to note that people do not come to therapy to remain the same. I keep the change in mind on a regular basis and by changing the thought processes and the words they use in that thought process, including the seven dirty words, you can really work on being more realistic and goal-orientated towards change. It is important to remember our thought processes are key to the change in our lives. Using the right words to get to where we want to be is probably one of the most important things to keep in mind. Thoughts guide the way we deal with things, and in changing those words, this can lead to the benefits of therapy in the long run.

Being able to work on your mind and your thought processes may be the most beneficial thing you could ever do for yourself and for your client. Do not be afraid of it, instead, embrace it. A great mind is a terrible thing to waste, so use it wisely.

Chapter 5: Body Language

Keywords: Competition with Self, Fitness, Flora Gut, Health, Journaling, Nutrition, Physical Injuries, Self-Esteem, Shoulds, TMS

It might seem strange for a therapist to talk about the body, as you go to a therapist for the health of your mind, not for a physical exam. To be a complete person, however, you need to also look at and be critical of your physical health, while working on your spirit and mind. In this chapter, I will discuss the importance of keeping the body in mind, no pun intended.

One of the things that I do when I start with a new client, besides the whole HIPAA compliance stuff that is *so* fun, *so* informative, so comprehensive, and incredibly boring, is discuss their last physical with their medical doctor or at any medical facility. It is important to know that date, as well as how it went and if there were any findings. I learned the importance of this issue the hard way when a close person in my life was diagnosed with a mental health issue without proper medical clearance.

The story goes that this person in my life, who I will refer to as 'J.Doe', started having issues with their mood. It was very apparent that things had changed, and I was struggling to deal with it. J.Doe was also angry and mean to those around them, and had difficulty staying awake during the day, but also struggled to sleep at nighttime. Feeling this way, they decided to consult a therapist as all they wanted is for things to stabilize. They went there, and a psychiatrist visit was suggested. At that time, they were suggested a powerful psychotropic medication to manage their mood.

J.Doe then went to see their medical doctor, as they felt unsure about taking a psychotropic and wanted to talk it over with a doctor they trusted. The doctor did a full lab markup, and, as she suspected, a few medical ailments were discovered. The doctor was not going to leave any stone unturned in order to make sure it was really a mental health ailment. Turns out, J.Doe had an undiagnosed, underactive thyroid, and that is why their mood was all over the place. After a few weeks on a thyroid medication,their mood stabilized, and they never had to take a psychotropic medication again in their life.

That is why I think it is essential to ask about previous medical examinations. If it has been a while since a patient has gone for a checkup, I look at the onset of the symptoms of mental health issues and if they occurred prior or post the reported date of the physical. You always want to make sure to not give a mental health diagnosis that can be cleared on a physiological level. Diagnosis can be perceived as a lifetime of suffering and not something a client may escape easily; despite anything you might say to reassure them.

Your body affects your mental health, and it is important for many people to understand that. If you have a physical ailment that will affect your mental health, we need to figure out how to treat that properly. Having a serious physical diagnosis can bring on a slew of mental health issues, including depression, anxiety, among others. It also may create some traumatic responses, as it may trigger memories of individuals, they know who were diagnosed with something similar. In many cases, it makes you believe that you are going to go through something similar.

I've experienced back pain for a long time in my life, but even after different treatments, it would always hurt at different times, whether I exercise or not. I then heard about Dr. John Sarno on the Howard Stern Show. His concept, Tension Myositis Syndrome (TMS), states that some of our physical pain may not be explained by structural abnormalities but may be due to psychological distress (33). Some may call it psychosomatic in our field (34). He concentrates specifically on back pain which really resonated to me. Once I started doing therapy and working on my issues, it helped. What I like to do when I have a back problem, is to start thinking of my interactions I had during the day and see if any made me feel uncomfortable. It also helps to look ahead to see if anything that is coming up in the next few days is making me feel uncomfortable. I journal about it, and it has been crucial to my physical recovery on a regular basis.

Most people with a physical diagnosis can also get better by doing simple things, such as doing physical activity that is not strenuous. While no one will dispute that going to the gym and working out can be beneficial to many people, it is something that some people simply aren't interested in. There are misconceptions on what a workout is, as well as what must be done to get better. There is also an intimidation factor that occurs with going to a gym and not being able to keep up. It is important to discuss all the options that a person may have. Many gyms offer trainers which can help.

When we talk about working out, people imagine marathoners, sports athletes, and other fitness gurus that have done fantastic things with those regiments. This can be intimidating to many and something that seems out of reach. While it is okay to look up to these athletes and other training and fitness individuals, it is also scary. Most people imagine working out twice everyday and still feeling they can't get to that level of 'perfection'. They give up before they even start.

Therapy can be beneficial to discuss what training really means. Starting slow and going at your own pace is key. Also, making sure that you are doing exercises that are within your capacity. If you have had a history of any back problems for example, there must be a discussion with your doctor regarding that. Same goes for any other types of presenting or past injuries. I like having this conversation with individuals because I like to set realistic goals.

It is also important to reach out to your doctor to make sure you know what you can and cannot do. It is also particularly important not to stress your body while pushing it. There is a delicate balance that as a therapist I cannot always understand but referring to professionals who do it is key. I also work with individuals who feel they must go all out on fitness to get to where they feel they should be, and age can play a factor. I also shiver when I hear people comparing themselves to others who are on social media or TV who are the same age and are in excellent shape. Fitspiration is a real, and very dangerous problem in our society.

This may seem counterintuitive but let me explain. The people they usually compare themselves to have done this for years and sometimes, that's their only job. They do not have the same day-to-day obligations than most of my clients must do. They have also been doing it for a long period of time, something that most of my clients have not done for years. It is important to pace yourself and find ways to reach them properly. Realistic goals are always the key.

I also see many fitness individuals who post many pictures of themselves on social media to show how their body has been shaped by working out and how their life has changed. While I do believe that this can happen, it can be discouraging for some. It could also be difficult to understand that their body shape and other factors play a role. If you cannot reach those goals, you start feeling down on yourself and give up on the workout. It also makes you feel like you will not be able to continue working out. What is the point, after all, if you feel that you will never be able to be like those individuals?

The effect of the working out can affect self-esteem. And not necessarily in a good way. If you follow some of these fitness individuals online, they will post pictures of themselves and/or others including clients and show how they have improved quickly and efficiently with some of the changes they suggest. The people I work with tend to compare themselves to these individuals and feel like they need to reach the same goals as those shown. Anything less can be seen by clients as a failure. When people feel like that, they do not want to continue.

I have many conversations with my clients to discuss how they need to set realistic goals and how things take time. No matter what your body type is, having a conversation about the improvements is key and while positivity is important, realism to me is much more important. Even if you read a "Couch to 5K" book word for word, that does not guarantee that you will be running a 5K by the end of the book. Maybe you do not have the right body type, maybe you lack interest, or maybe physical issues that will prevent you from doing that. Other factors can play a role also.

I have a client who could not run for the life of him. He tried everything and was constantly getting injured or feeling discouraged by his outcomes. We worked on many things, one of which included the fact that he pushed himself because he thought he "should" be at certain points at certain times. Discussing different body types as well as abilities was key there. It was also important to discuss that the competition that most people have is with themselves, not others.

I started running about seven years ago and while I have run two half marathons, I have never won any! The reason why I say that is because some people feel that they must be the best and anything less than that is a failure. The fact that I went from not being able to run 250 feet without being out of breath at 265 pounds to a half marathon was my accomplishment. I did not finish at the top of any of my half marathons. The fact that I was able to do it was what I really appreciated. I also was happy that on my second one, I beat the time of my first one.

When you compete with yourself, it can only push you to get better. Sure, you cannot always beat yourself in every run, as there are multiple factors that also play a factor there, including the weather as well as what is going on mentally and physically with you. The fact is that I do my best, which is what keeps me going. I recently hurt my knee and going back to running has been a humbling experience, but I continue doing it despite not having done the miles or speed that I used to. The fact that I am still doing it is the true accomplishment.

Another important factor to consider in your body is your nutrition. This is another thing that I have seen on social media that seems to go to extremes. They also show the loss of weight as well as other stuff that have improved people's lives once they start changing, including inches lost, more muscle tone, etc. and it all seems to happen quickly. The fact is that it takes time, and a change in nutrition that extreme can also be detrimental. I will not point fingers at any particular diet but at the end of the day, I encourage one specific type of diet: common sense and moderation.

About three years ago, I received a certificate in diet and nutrition, and it was very eye-opening. While I do not want to speak as if I'm an expert, the one thing that I got from the certificate program is that a specific diet does not work, because an exclusion of any type can be detrimental if you don't supplement elsewhere. If you exclude certain things, you may see a loss of weight and inches but as soon as you reintroduce that element, the weight comes back quickly(35). Your body does not need all the nutrition it can get and learning how to do it using moderation and common sense is key.

How do you moderate? Well, one of the best ways to moderate is to eat slower. One of the bad habits that most people have is to consume their food or beverages quickly. Let us do an exercise: what did you eat for lunch yesterday? How did it taste? What texture did it have? Was there a particular spice that was in there? If you can answer that question, you are much better than most people. Most people barely remember what they ate, and they do not concentrate on the texture or what they enjoyed about it. If you take time to taste your food, it will also make you feel fuller. And with time, you will notice the change in your body.

I have also been reading *A Mind of Your Own* by Kelly Brogan (36). This book is fascinating, and it certainly has impacted a little bit of what I have done, not only in my practice but in my own life as well. This is all thanks to a friend of mine. She went through some difficulties in her life and decided to look at this book as an alternative to medications. It talked about the floral gut and how important it is to maintain it. It also discussed different things about how our dietary choices play a factor in our behavior, as well as how our body reacts to these choices.

One of the things that has helped is to introduce probiotics in my life. While I am just a therapist and I am not endorsing you to change your nutrition without consulting a doctor and nutritionist, I found it helpful in my own life. I have also used different medications to address any inflammations that I have. While there is a craze of gluten-free diets, this book showed me how gluten inflames parts of your body which may also make you feel physically exhausted, as well as inflame your stomach. It also talks about making sure that you have a balanced diet without overeating and addressing different types of nutrients that are essential.

I once heard that diet and exercise should no longer be used. It should be nutrition and healthy physical habits. I like that a whole lot better, and it seems a lot more realistic. We have some preconceived notions on what diet and exercise is and by changing the name, it may be easier for people to adapt to that lifestyle and those choices. It is important to realize that it will not happen overnight and will take time. Having these new habits will probably help in the long run. The rule that I have heard is that you will feel the change within four weeks, it will show physically after eight, and people will notice after 12 weeks.

Now how does this relate to mental health? Well, when you start feeling better about your eating habits, you will have psychological benefits because of your new, healthy ways of life. it will help you feel better about yourself and realize that, like anything else, it will take some time and hard work will pay off. Mentally, people can really relate to that. Our bodies are adaptable and realizing that they adapt with time is key.

The other thing that I like to talk about is muscle testing with my clients. This is not an exercise thing, but rather about what your body knows before your mind does. Kinesiology is described as functional neurology and has been part of some of the more eclectic approaches in therapy (37). I learned how to use it while training in the Brain Fit Academy (38). You can ask for the assistance from another to do it, and you can also do it on your own.

The exercise I typically do with my clients is as follows: ask permission to touch their arms and if they agree, I ask them to close their eyes and think of something they are confident about. I then ask them to put their arms up straight forward and to resist me pushing down their arms as much as they can. Then, I ask them to put their arms down for a few seconds and think of something they feel they want to improve. I then ask them to raise their arms and resist me as much as they can while I push down on their arms.

Result? The arm strength is significantly better when they are confident versus when they are not. Why do this exercise? It can indicate certain things in their lives. I like to use this exercise for those who struggle with chatting in therapy, feel too exposed, or are unsure of what they think on certain subjects and things in their lives. It demonstrates that they do know the answer deep down inside. If we redo the test on certain things they are questioning in their lives, it can help the patient figure out what they want to do with it. You can also do it with both your hands, and while using your thumb and index finger, you can ask yourself a question and try to separate your two hands with your thumb and index finger interlocked in a ring formation.

We all have some body knowledge of ourselves and sometimes, our bodies know the answer before we do. It is important to really listen to your body in that way. I also discuss how we need to stop eating when we feel full, as your body is telling you that you do not need any more food, or to listen to our "gut" instinct. If something makes our stomach or other parts of our body feel unsettled, your body is telling you something about the situation or the person you are interacting with at the time.

While most of my clients are readily willing to acknowledge that there is "women's intuition", I do believe men also have that instinctive knowledge, but they are usually not attuned to it. Maybe it is socialization. Maybe it is because it is not as clear for men as women but ultimately, both have access to that and need to realize that their body is also trying to tell them something about it.

Our sense of sight can also tell us a whole lot more about others, as well as how we are feeling. Body language has been studied extensively, but it is also one of the most underused abilities we all have. My clients sometimes become annoyed with me, as I note body movement, as well as their eye contact as indicators of how they truly feel about certain things.

While this book is not meant to be a body language course, I like to use eye contact as well as the crossing/uncrossing of arms and legs with individuals as a way to get a sense of how they truly feel. Please understand that I assume my clients are telling me the truth about how they feel and how they express it. I do use body language as an indicator, as it can sometimes be a wealth of information in regards to their true feelings about different things.

I will use easy examples that most know but do not always use. The first one is the crossing and uncrossing of the arms and legs. It is not a 100% science, but it tends to be fairly accurate and an indicator of a person's true feelings. By crossing their arms and legs, it shows a closure to certain things and noting that behavior is key as a therapist(39). You will see that this is also important in your day-to-day life with different people.

Another example is the gaze of the eyes. While it is not always accurate, I can observe my clients to see if they are telling me the truth by asking them what they had for breakfast that morning or where they had for supper the night before. Watching where they look is key to figure out which way they will tend to gaze to tap their memory. Most people do not want to lie about their previous supper or their breakfast in the morning. This is typically used to address a client's true feelings about different things.

I also like to look for what Paul Ekman has called micro-expressions (40). We can discuss different types, but the ones I look for is shame as well as when they discuss certain things, particularly interactions with others. This is important for me to note as it indicates more issues with those individuals, and a need to be explored in more depth. Most clients are honest but sometimes, we become uncomfortable bad mouthing our parents for example. Those micro-expressions become key to identify the true issues.

With time, I also note some confidence posturing by my clients. One of the signs was their hands behind their head either interlocked or not. It showed an openness as well as more confidence in what they are doing. They will also tend to look you in the eye and smile. While body language is not an exact science, it is a definite way to see tendencies and what people are doing regarding their emotions and feelings.

Between nutrition, our three parts of our brain, as well as our gut instinct, I do believe we are able to understand more of what is going on, and need to realize that our body is not only a vessel, but a wealth of information.

Chapter 6: Look Up to the Spirit in Your Life

Keywords: Belief System, Buddhism, Change, Distractions, Gratitude, Meditation, Mindfulness, Prayer, Religion, Science

Spirituality has received some negative connotations over the years. Certainly something that is treated like a taboo word is better left to organized religion, and never to be spoken about in family or holiday gatherings, right? It invokes mostly this intense practice of praying or meditating and is linearity and divisive.

While spirituality is not something that I bring up first in my conversation with my clients, I do bring it up in any way I can. One of the ways that I bring it up is to discuss the belief system of individuals. It is important to have that discussion, as it is not simply what religion you are, but rather what is your set of beliefs regarding your spiritual side.

There have been times in my life where I felt that if you did not believe in the scientific value of research, that you did not base your life on true research, and things that can be put in a box, then religion is obviously not what you believe in. It is easy to fall into that thought process when everyone around you finds a way to destroy any belief that you may have, simply because it creates so much tension. In other words, if I know something I say/believe may cause tension, I would rather not talk about it and let it be, then try to explore what it truly means to me.

Let me start off by saying that I consider myself a recovering Catholic. This is by no means a way to be derogatory towards the Catholic religion or any religion for that matter. I grew up in a very Catholic upbringing in Canada, particularly Québec. Until the early 1960s, it could be argued that religion controlled most things in that province. We still grew up in the 70s and 80s with schools that were mostly Catholic and had religious teachings. After all, my first principal was an actual nun!

My mom was Catholic and my dad was Protestant but when they got married, my dad was told that I had to be brought up Catholic. They did not impose religion on me whatsoever but felt it was important that I do the rites of passage, whether it is baptism, communion, confirmation, and such. I never took to the system itself, as I felt it was very rigid and had limited space for questioning or discussing different things. In fact, one of my Catholic teachers had asked me to stop asking questions regarding Catholic beliefs!

I do not mean to be negative about Catholic beliefs, but I say that I am recovering as I did not identify much with the religious system. I say that I am in recovery, as I sometimes slip and say, "Oh My God" as well as "Jesus Christ." The swears in Québec (both in French and English) are all based on Catholic paraphernalia. I guess that is why I will always be in recovery, as I have slips here and there. Overall, I do believe that there is some good in that religion, and I hope that anyone reading this who may be offended understands that it is not meant to demean Catholicism.

Today, I went from a person who did not believe in anything, to a person who likes to take beliefs from different religions and put them in place in my own personal life. If I had to identify to one religion, I would say that I identify to Buddhist principles, as Buddhism is not considered a religion. I do believe in the Four Noble Truths, as well as the eightfold path to enlightenment (41). I also meditate every night. I have read many of the Buddhist teachings and really feel that they are something to be followed. Understand that by saying this, I also recognize that this is not the only way to believe in spirituality.

I once belonged to a Unitarian/Universalist congregation. The belief system that they have, accepting all religions and all beliefs and being open to different views without imposing them on others, is truly something that makes sense to me. It is considered a covenant and an agreement among all parishioners to discuss different things and have an open mind. They have been there for me when I had some difficulties , and my Reverend walked me through it. I will be forever grateful to him and that parish.

Why am I saying all this? I want you to understand that, at one point, I was a human being that felt that religion was not for the strong minded, it was a way for the weak minded to be trained. Thankfully, people change with time and I have learned to embrace different types of belief systems, something that I am proud that I have done. I am certainly never going to deny who I was, but the good news is, all humans can change including me. This is a principal that I bring to any spiritual discussion with my clients.

I do believe that being able to join others in their beliefs while also having an open discussion without imposing your thoughts on others is key. It is difficult to find this type of conversation nowadays, especially with recent issues with all of nothing thinking, but it is key to bring it up in order to be receptive to others. I also like to link this discussion to another great spiritual practice that has changed my life - mindfulness and meditation.

These two practices come from Buddhist principles. It is a spiritual belief system based on traditions, values, and practices based on the original teachings of Buddha. Depending on what source you read, Buddha lived around 2500 to 3000 years ago and had a very privileged life. Born a prince, he lived in luxury, shielded from the world, until he decided to leave his previous life behind. He decided, at his parents' great chagrin, to go live in the community, and created many of these principles. While I can go on and on about Buddhism, I just want to give you some ideas of what a practice based on those principles may look like.

Buddha would not want us to discuss it as a religion, although many people will recognize it as religion. He has talked about four principles of Buddhism. The first one is that life is suffering and when you think about it, it makes perfect sense. Life is not easy, and he recognizes that. He does also recognize what brings suffering in this life. The second principle then ascertains that life is suffering due to desire and how our desires sometimes get in the way of a happier life. The third principle talks about how to get to a happier life by not clinging or attaching to anything. And how do you get there? That is the fourth principle which is the eightfold path to enlightenment.

The eightfold path to enlightenment (also called the Middle Way) states the following. You need to find the following:

Right View

Right Insight

Right Speech

Right Attitude

Right Livelihood

Right Mindfulness

Right Effort

Right Concentration

I can go on about Buddhism but I would rather suggest that you pick up a good book on this subject, I would read *Awakening the Buddha Within*, written brilliantly and wisely by Lama Surya Das(42). It makes Buddhism very accessible and really had a great impact in my spiritual practice.

Getting back to mindfulness and meditation, my life is changed for the better by meditating every night. I think that we need to realize that meditating is not what we see on TV or what you would expect from a Buddhist monk. Meditation is a lot more accessible and easier for many people if you follow some simple principles. If you want to try it, take two or three minutes and close your eyes. You do not need to breathe at any pace, instead just concentrate on your breathing. Take note where it goes in or where it goes out. Just notice your breath. It keeps your mind from being distracted and thinking about other things. Being able to do that for about three minutes is easy. You can use a timer or stopwatch. This is your first quick lesson on meditation.

While I have simplified an extraordinarily complex subject, I just think that sometimes, people try to make meditation more than it is. The principle is that you do not let your mind wander to other things. You concentrate on one singular thing which is your breath. Currently, our minds can be all over the place, even before bed. Many people who report poor sleep and issues with anxiety prior or while lying in bed have tried to learn how to do meditation; that has made things a lot easier for them and made them feel less anxious prior to bed. It is not a cure-all by any stretch, but it does help get you back in the moment.

The other practice that I talk about is mindfulness. This is another subject that has many complex meanings, but it can be simplified so that you can practice it on a day-to-day basis. Mindfulness is defined as a state of mind where you are conscious or aware of something. One of the easiest ways that I ask my clients to practice mindfulness is to take a few minutes a day to not play with their phone, and just notice one thing. Perhaps it is at a coffee shop. Notice the smells and not judge them. Or perhaps it is hearing a sound of something that you never notice. I like to refer to someone's refrigerator or heating/cooling system. The goal is to pay attention to one thing at a time. Doing this for 2 to 3 minutes a day will also calm you down.

This spiritual practice has helped me in several ways. It keeps me from getting frazzled when lots of things are going on. It also makes me concentrate on the things I can control versus things I cannot control.

When I feel out of control, being able to control my thoughts by paying attention to one thing at a time is immensely helpful. It also reminds me that there is only one thing that can be done at a time. And if you pay attention to it, you will do it well. The more you do it, the more you will be less distracted and the more you will be effective at doing those two or three different things at the same time.

I like to state to my clients; "Imagine if during counseling I was paying attention to two or three other things while I am talking to you. By being in the moment, it makes me a much more effective therapist." That does not mean that nothing else is going on in my life and that there are no other things that will bother me later on, but that is because I'm with this one person at that moment, it makes it a lot easier to just concentrate on what they are doing. It is spiritually important to connect with the individual that is in front of you, not let yourself be distracted by other things that may be happening in your professional or private life. Clients tend to really relate to that and appreciate that you also practice something that you might ask them to do later on.

While I talk about Buddhism heavily here, please understand that all religions are effective for many people. One of the other practices that I discussed with my clients is prayer. This is a universal practice in the spiritual world and I certainly encourage individuals to do so. It is important to look at prayer to be thankful for what you have, as well as to be grateful for your current life. While some individuals will ask for things through prayer and that is okay, I believe that prayer of gratitude is the most effective to realize what you have and not what you don't have.

Spiritually, it is hard to be thankful sometimes. There are so many things going on in this world that it is difficult to think about other stuff. But if you are able to realize what you have, be grateful for that, and concentrate on the moment versus what might happen in the future or remind yourself of the negative stuff from the past, you may be able to realize what you're working towards. We are all linked on some level or another. Learning how to be grateful in the moment with what you have may help you realize how we have more similarities than differences with other people. And if you realize that, you may not concentrate on all the things you do not have.

I also encourage people to do things that are fulfilling for them. I talked about how most people that, at the end of their life, do not talk about the riches they have or how much more they had than others. Most people, on their deathbed, want to really connect with others. The biggest regret that I hear is that they did not get close to their own family, friends, community, or others in the world. We spend so much time worrying about what needs to be happening next that we lose sight of who we have and what we have in front of us. Being able to connect with one single human being is quite a gift. That doesn't mean we will get along with everyone nor do we need to connect with everyone, but that's because of our similarities across most humans, we may be able to understand a lot more of others when we connect with them.

A final note on spirituality: whether you believe in an afterlife, believe in a higher power, or think that we are dust at the end of the day, all these things are spiritual practices. Thinking that we are all done after life is over and that there are no gods, no afterlife, or no reincarnations, that is a spiritual practice. How so? If this is the only life you got, what are you going to do with it? It is important to realize that this is all we have right now. We can only control the present and being able to do it in a spiritual way, mindfully and respectfully towards other humans, is key for our own mental health well-being.

Spirituality is a universal trait that we must all realize. The differences that we have, which are generally small, should be celebrated in order to realize that different beliefs may help the health of individuals in the same way.

Chapter 7: Addiction Treatment

Keywords: Detoxification, Education, Forced Choice, Medication Assisted Treatment (MAT), Mental Health, Nonjudgmental, Overdoses, Self-Help (AA, NA, SMART, etc.) Substances

Becoming involved with addiction treatment was something I would call a "happy accident", because to this day, I continue to enjoy it. When I received my master's, I started off in the field of emergency/correctional mental health. I unfortunately had a negative outcome in the correctional setting that was difficult to comprehend for me. I also had a similar experience on the crisis side of things. This made me rethink the type of work I wanted to do. I ended up continuing in the emergency department for another eight years part time, but that's a different story for a different day.

Let me start this chapter by letting you know one of my biggest pet peeves in my field. I hear this all the time from my colleagues, both from within the state and outside it. It drives me mad because at the basis, it is not true at all. The statement: "I don't treat substance abuse" is a plain lie. While I understand not everyone is trained specifically for that specialty, to think that you do not treat substance use issues is a fallacy that you are telling yourself.

Let me bore you with facts to start off. Individuals who are diagnosed with mental health issues are twice as likely to have a substance use issue than the general population (43). The reverse is also true. Most individuals who abuse substances tend to use it to cope with a mental health disorder. Those who struggle with mental health disorders tend to use substances to make the unpleasant symptoms of their disorder disappear. The facts are that you likely treat both.

More importantly, substance use affects just about everyone in the population. If you look at recent trends around substance use (which includes alcohol, THC, and illegal and prescription drugs), you can see that, at any time, 34.5% of the population has had an abuse issue in their lifetime (44). Add that to the facts above, this shows that it affects everyone, and it means we all at least know someone with an issue with substances.

Substance use has always been difficult to address, as most individuals in the general population see substance use as a choice, something a person does on a volunteer basis. While It is partly true, as the first use is based on the choices of the individual, it is also something that becomes less of a choice with time. In my experience, the first try tends to be a choice but after a while, you tend to use it in order to just keep the symptoms of withdrawal at bay. You also feel embarrassment, that you cannot reach out, as we stigmatize substance use and how we "choose" to be addicted.

I also find it disheartening when I hear people talk about the choice a person made and how it is poor judgement or the wrong thing. While I have treated this for over 20 years, either professionally or in my private life, I have never met an addict who woke up one day and stated: "Gee let us get addicted today. What is out there that is considered wrong and difficult to stop suddenly?" It is a fallacy that people choose this lifestyle. They usually do not want to be addicted; they want to talk about it, but who is safe to confide in?

Family members may be well intended, but what do they do to make sure the person can talk to them about it and safely reach out? I think most families do not know how to deal with substance abuse and addiction issues, so they struggle as to "what to do" in these situations. Defaulting to not knowing and blaming the person struggling with addiction is simpler than informing themselves or admitting not knowing in most of the cases. It is faster and makes some families move on easier from the person, to protect themselves.

When family members ask me how to deal with substance use, I need to ask them the most difficult, and the most uncomfortable question they are going to hear: "Does the person want the help?" Family members are sometimes ready to get help for the individual before the person who is addicted is ready themselves. It is difficult, because some family members have been through hell and back with the family member, trying to help them. But the ultimate responsibility lies solely on the person who has an addiction issue.

So, what can you do to help those with addiction issues? Many things. The first thing is to listen without judgement or prejudice. If a person is opening about their addiction, let them talk. Do not ask the why right away, as they probably do not even know why. They also may be embarrassed, so being able to talk about it is certainly a huge first step for them. It is key to show support. Asking for help is never easy for anyone, never mind when it is related to addiction, something we tend to stigmatize way too much anyway.

Be willing to learn. While you may never have an addiction issue (I believe we are all addicted to something, but that is a discussion for somewhere else), you do not know what it is to remain sober or away from your addiction for that particular individual. Be curious, ask them what they have tried, and if anything, what has worked and what has not worked. It may be informative for you as well as for them. It is a good way to know what could work. It is also helpful to not offer things they feel has not worked already. Do not offer advice unless they ask directly. It is important, mostly because they may feel advice as judgement on your part.

The other way to help is to get informed properly. Do not turn to "Googling it", as a way to deal with their issue. While Google has been a great help for several things, including news, sharing, shopping, and connecting with others, the misinformation that is available on Google can lead well-intended individuals to find information that may not be helpful. Think about medical symptoms you have googled (let's face it, we have all done this) and how many times did it give you a horrific disease list? And long before you googled treatment on these diseases? Well, it can be quite overwhelming. So, imagine someone who has limited knowledge on an addiction looking for the answer on treatment and solution.

Many of the links that are offered at the top of the webpage are usually paid content. They offer "guaranteed" results with certain treatments. And for the modest price of $20,000, you can have access to it too. Just like they teach you in school, if it is too good to be true, it probably is. Treatment centers, 1-800 numbers, herbal remedies are all offered when you simply Google any type of substance use treatment. While I cannot say they do not all work, it may be time to get a little more savvy on treatment considerations.

The first thing I suggest is to make sure you find reliable websites. The use of .org may have been offered to the general population for quite some time, but they tend to also be used by better suited organizations. .edu are usually education based and can be a good source of information, as well as the best course of treatment. They also may link you to reputable services. If you do not find those sites helpful, it may be time to call in the insurance companies.

While we are mandated to have health insurance at this time in this country (this is written in 2020), many do not have health insurance. While the person you want to help may not have insurance, health insurances in your specific state will be able to point you in the right direction for treatment. They probably have a list of treatment centers/detoxes available if you call them or on their website. These places tend to be regulated in some way and be a good starting point. I tend to start off at their website just to make sure.

Otherwise, SAMHSA has a help line for treatment of addictions (as well as mental health). They are funded via the federal government and they tend to have great resources for you. Their number is 1-800-662-HELP. It is a 24/7 line. Most areas in the United States also have a crisis team available to them 24/7. While some offer evaluations and some may only be open specific hours, they usually have the most accurate information on the best treatment in the area you live in. They are not typically sponsored by any company, so they will give you a list of resources you may be able to use.

Another great way to get support on addictions is through self-help programs. While most have a perception of AA, NA, CA, SMART, and other substance related self-help groups, remind yourself that they will have a list of supports for you, including the next steps for you. I would suggest you reach out to those organizations for a more realistic view of what they do. Self-help groups vary from region to region, including which ones are available, what their emphasis is, as well as geographical reachability. It is important to realize what is best for the person also. Their perception plays a huge factor on treatment. Again, make sure they can choose what they want versus imposing "what works".

I have been hearing about self-help for 30+ years and I certainly have had a perception of what "they do" that has changed significantly. When I first heard of them, it was mostly through my mother who was an HR director in a telecommunications company. She had talked about workers there having substance use issues and needing to go to meetings to get treatment and support for their problems with substances. Little did I know it was not "treatment" at the time or how it worked. I knew they did 12 steps and they knew what to do. Based on that limited knowledge, I figured it was sufficient and that people all got better if they went.

Eventually, after going to college and university, I learned more about the 12-step tradition. It really rubbed me the wrong way for several reasons. First, it was not actual treatment, and it was others with the same problem helping those who came to meetings. In my 19-20-year-old mind, I wondered how that would actually work. It made no sense to me. If everyone there had a problem, how could they "solve" it for others struggling?

Then there was the higher power stuff that I really disliked. As mentioned previously, I was a full-blown recovering Catholic and with that label, I was opposed to any type of God. I was an atheist at the time and no imaginary person could help individuals to recover, let alone could give them their power! It was unheard of for me and felt it was craziness at its best! I could never send someone there. And there weren't many robust studies about self-help. The methodology was either flawed or done with self-reports. No way was this any good.

Then, I went to meetings with my clients. That was eye opening. Clients kept telling me it does not work, that they were told not to take their medications for significant mental health issues, as this is considered chewing your drug, that people would use these meetings to get to tell their glory day stories, or that you had to recite "cult like" the serenity prayer. I was skeptical to say the least based on that information. When I attended, I saw many truths in what was told to me and I did not like it one bit.

This story has changed again since then. After attending a few open meetings (closed are only for those who are in the program), I saw some of the exaggerations that my clients had fed me. It did help that I also went with some clients that were several years clean thanks to Bill W's program. I saw the feelings of community, the spirit of the program, and how that can guide many in the right way. I also saw some meetings in which my clients' words on AA were true. Confused and unsure, I read a little more.

Learning the 12 steps is hard. I felt it was heavy reading, and truly did not like the structure of some of the stuff. And that higher power stuff, despite my Buddhist principles, was for the birds. I really tried to understand it more but did not feel it would be for everyone. I would recommend the groups and see if a client felt it was right for them. If it were not, I would recommend other self-help groups and other options. I was not convinced that this was what my clients truly needed on a day to day basis and never forced attendance (other than when I was working during my parole and probation days, when they could mandate it. Thankfully, it cannot be mandated anymore).

So today, 2020, I am now a strong supporter of the self-help groups, *if* the client is willing to attend and do the work. I don't force it, but I certainly see the value of it much clearer than ever before. So why the change of heart? Russell Brand. Yes, the actor, comic, and sometimes political activist. In 2018, I read the book "Recovery" which he penned(45). He was guided through his 12 steps by a freaking Atheist! Can you believe it? Read the book, it is awesome. What he did with the book was to make the steps much more palpable to me, and I have given several copies so far too many of my clients. He dissects the step in a reachable way and makes it easier to answer the questions to move you forward.

I want to add an extra step, common to many of my clients in recovery: it is something that happens with many individuals who are sober in the long-term. I call it the "now what?" stage. One of the things that happens with the 12 steps is that if you do them all, you should feel better right? Well sometimes, there is a big letdown after those 12 steps. When people start, there is a lot of encouragement, but as a person goes through the steps, other than their sponsor, there is less support and it becomes assumed that they are doing well. That is why the "now what?" step exists for me. My clients typically tell me that they have done everything they were supposed to and sometimes, they do not feel better. Now what?

This is where it is important to support the client and validate their experience. It is both scary and lonely to be at that step. I do believe that is why many people continue to go to meetings after they are done with the 12 steps. Offering support with a recap of their accomplishments and explaining that they can do many other things that they could not do under the influence is helpful. As Russell Brand said, he re-does the 12 steps on a regular basis.

The other treatment that I recommend is Medication Assisted Treatment programs or MAT. This was and still is, a touchy subject. I came to know more about its effectiveness when I was on a task force for opioid overdose prevention in 2009. Before I was asked to attend this first meeting, I had taken the law enforcement point of view at the time of MAT: if it is a controlled substance, it cannot be ingested. My self-help folks can relate right? After all, you don't chew your drug, do you? I did not agree with mental health medications being restricted, but to restrict methadone and suboxone? Sure thing. They are opioids after all.

Obviously, we all evolved and the meeting was quite enlightening. The group aimed to lower accidental deaths from opioid/opiate overdoses by using Narcan. Narcan was not as easily accessed in 2008 and the work group aimed to add it to all ambulance, police, and firefighter vehicles in order to prevent overdoses. There was resistance at the time from certain first responders groups but today, it is part of the equipment of first responders' vehicles. It was also helpful, as it helped demystify the view that overdoses were unpreventable. We were able to reduce the number of fatal overdoses over the next 10 years and help other cities and towns understand the importance of Narcan.

At this same first meeting, there was a great presentation on how to use MAT to reduce the number of overdoses. This presentation explained how detoxes can be very scary, as the withdrawal symptoms can be difficult. Individuals who struggled with opioid dependence would rather use than go through that. Especially that getting a detox bed was not an easy task. MAT was a great way to avoid some withdrawals symptoms and most importantly, we knew what was in those medications. One of the other fatal overdoses occurred when the street drugs were laced with other drugs. As you may know, drugs sold on the street are not FDA approved and there is no guarantee that the drugs may not include other things, including the coating of pills.

I took this great information and helped create a policy with the law enforcement agency I was working at the time. This policy was able to allow individuals who struggled with addiction, either currently or in the past, get on an MAT in order to manage their addiction. It resulted in less fatal overdoses and individuals who were willing to do the work to remain sober via the MAT. We worked to create relationships in the community with prescribers to move toward a better understanding on both the public health and the public safety components of this epidemic, which led to better collaboration in the long term.

Methadone, suboxone, and Vivitrol are the names most associated with MAT. Methadone is an agonist, which means it mimics opiates/opioids in their component. Suboxone/Subutex is a partial agonist which means it partially blocked the opiate receptors while still containing an amount of opiate/opioid. Vivitrol is an antagonist, which means it blocks the opioid receptor completely and contains no opioid. Which one is better? Not for me to decide. When an individual struggling with addiction is seeking help, limiting which MAT can be as damaging, as they feel again, out of control. When you give choices to individuals, they tend to be more receptive to treatment and feedback. As my good friend stated: "Let's not forget about the A(ssisted) in MAT.

Other MATs exist for other addictions, so feel free to talk to your medical professional about it. They can guide you on the subject. With the support of a therapist, which I feel is imperative in the MAT programming, individuals can be better equipped to work on their recovery and realize the reasons for their initial attraction to those drugs. I feel we may not always see it, but there is always a thought process that leads to use. Having a clearer head, with the help of MAT, will help move individuals to better coping mechanisms in the long run. Giving individuals the responsibility and control with their recovery will benefit them in the long run.

I took the point of view of an outpatient provider on this subject but obviously there are many other medical ways to address addiction. Detoxes come to mind. I also believe that intensive outpatient programs, rehabilitation centers, long term residential programs, and sober housing are also important.

Because of my limited knowledge on the subjects, I'd rather deferred that information to someone else.

Recovery happens every day, and by giving individuals the strength and resources to go forward may be the best way to go.

Chapter 8: The Unique Challenges of First Responders, Dispatchers, and Correctional Staff

Keywords: Culture, Cognitive Distortions, Defunding, Disconnect, Dispatch, Diversion, Fire, Jail, Police, Stigma, Trauma, Validation

When I started my first job as a master's level job, I always thought I would end up working outpatient and the crisis team. After all, I really wanted to sit there with individuals who sought counseling for their problems. I did not realize that the company I worked for did not have any full time openings in those settings. I will always be grateful they wanted me to work with them full-time, but the opening they eventually had was in a setting I had not really thought about: the criminal justice setting. While I always believed it was the future of treatment, this was not the plan I had. It ended up creating a passion for treating an underserved population: those who work in correctional settings, as well as first responders.

It all started with my work with the crisis team and the Jail Diversion Program, where we were helping divert the individual with mental health issues or substance use issues from the judicial setting. This was a part of the work that I enjoyed as a triage coordinator and with on-call work, I ended up doing more work on the diversion program with the local police officers. I also worked inside the jails as a mental health worker, where I performed support for inmates with mental health issues or evaluated those on suicide watch. I also was part of the first substance abuse coordinators at Massachusetts State Parole. I helped develop a comprehensive substance use and mental health assessment. In the formative years, we were learning what was important for those who are incarcerated and their return to the community.

I looked at the key components from the perspective of research already done by other resources in the United States. After all, if we were to help them reintegrate the community and avoid the staggering recidivism rate at the time, all information would be helpful. The evaluation that I developed during that time was very comprehensive and looked at their life situation, not only their substance use history or mental health. Looking at the whole picture was important. This also guided my work in Drug (now known with the more respectable name Recovery) Courts during this time.

We were also close to the correctional staff and worked hand in hand with them. This helped me understand more of the stressors they face. It was a great lesson on how institutional settings work, their paramilitary setting, as well as the complex relationship between the staff, inmates, the community portrayal of these institutions, as well as government pressures to meet criteria they had to uphold. I also was able to work with great nurses who also taught me about the stressors they face. This was also related to my work in the emergency services setting.

.

I learned about the difficulties they face in their own private lives, as well as the things they see change in their own mindset. Some officers are very cognizant of the daily routines and its effect on them, while others tend to try to bury it. This could lead to several problems and it was stuff that, again, I had never thought about. It was clear that they needed a different type of treatment if they were to reach out to a counselor, as the "touchy feely" approach may not have been, shall we say, appropriate?

I also was able to work with first responders throughout all this work. Whether it is police, fire, dispatch, or EMTS/Paramedics, they tend to see lots of things that most people do not know or do not want to know. Having minimally experienced it myself while I was with them, I can see why sometimes they tend to disconnect from their work. In some ways, it can be healthy, but it can also be problematic in their day to day lives, whether it is at work or at home. When you disconnect from a part of your life, it can be very tempting to disconnect in other ways as a protective behavior.

Trauma is a powerful thing of course, but also seeing sometimes how destructive human nature can be is probably the hardest part. It is an incredibly unique work where you run towards problems and need to make split decisions which could impact your life. That comes with lots of pressure. Not to mention how much the public tends to be negative in regards to them. It has been an exceedingly difficult time to be a police officer in the past few years.

This leads to a slew of problems: posttraumatic stress disorder, substance abuse, anxiety disorders, and that's just to name a few. First responders do not want to necessarily talk about these issues because it is not in the culture of their work. You are supposed to be able to let it go and move on because that is the nature of the work. While lots have been said about CISM (Critical Incident Stress Management) and its variant (Critical Incident Stress Debriefing or CISD) and their benefits(46), some individuals can choose to shut down at these debriefings due to several factors. Regardless, the ability to let them know they can reach out to a counselor that they can relate to has been very important. Knowing that a therapist does not get offended easily, as well as understands the nature of their work has been key to my success with working with this population.

Having also worked in an incarcerated setting, I tend to work with many correctional officers and others who have worked in a jail. It is again a unique situation to be in. One of the things that most people do not recognize is that jail is a different culture altogether. Whatever you know about jails from movies, it is usually not even close. But it is a different culture. Not only with the inmates being among themselves, but surprisingly correctional officers tend to be ridiculously hard on each other. Let's also remember that correctional staff are also surrounded by a criminal subculture in those settings. To paraphrase what the sheriff in Maricopa County once said: "The community deals with any individual who commits a crime for 6 seconds,6 minutes or 6 hours. We deal with them 6 months to 6 years, depending on their sentence". Again, my way of working with them has always been to meet them where they are at and discuss where their stressors are that they are willing to discuss.

The following paragraphs are also true for police officers and other first responders. The stressors they face every day are not very much different then everyone's life. They just happen to have a position where they are the authority. This is not exactly an extremely comfortable position for some of them. While they are OK with the extra responsibility, sometimes that extra responsibility comes with a lot of weight. For example, they need to get along with their coworkers but sometimes, they do this at their own expense. To get by for example, they may need to paint how they deal with certain things in a certain way when the authority or a coworker deal with it differently. They feel very conflicted regarding these compromises, especially in a job where compromise can be difficult.

They also must deal with a paramilitary structure. While it is OK to have that, it is sometimes very political in some places. For example, you may not agree with the person in charge, or you feel the other person's not done as much work as you have in the field. This makes for very tense situations. I also find that people with more experience in correctional settings struggle with people who have not been there as long as they have.

Conflict resolution is much different in these systems. While there is a structure in place for most of them, it is not typically how you deal with problems. Some want to deal with the problem 1 on 1 and not involve others, while others want to go through the chain of command. This also causes an "old school versus new school" mentality. While they are mostly on the same page, there is also space where they are not. They feel different in specific situations and unfortunately, they do not deal with small problems when that occurs.

I talked to my clients in regards to conflict resolution as a communication issue. Meeting someone's ability to resolve conflict is the first step. Realizing that they may deal with conflict in a different way is the second step. Finding ways to get to a point where each other understands is difficult. Lots of the communication that I discuss has a lot to do with cognitive distortions, especially not falling in all or nothing thinking. This is easier said than done for some. After all, they have been in this field for so long, and they have survived this way, why would they change?

Ultimately, it is learning to not be set in our ways and being able to be open minded. Some structures have been there forever and may change suddenly. Being flexible and understanding that the new way is just that, not to judge it is important in part of the job. They also have a great ability to discuss these issues with each other outside the job, but this can also be problematic.

Because of their particularly difficult jobs, they sometimes feel that only others who do the same job can understand them. Obviously, they come to learn that this is not necessarily true but because of that, they start doing things they probably would not have done otherwise. This is not because they are bad people, but there is something about having commonality that makes you feel you can do things that maybe others cannot. This holds particularly true for former combat veterans.

This also includes substance use. We have discussed at length substance use and the issues that this brings in a previous chapter. Ultimately, being able to relax seems to be related to substances for some. This becomes even more problematic when it is the only way to deal with things. They have difficult jobs that people don't really think about on a day-to-day basis. Sometimes it is glorified by others but ultimately, it can be stressful to do the work they do.

Substance abuse happens for different reasons, from a way to relax, to dealing with compassion fatigue, and vicarious trauma. While they may not be traumatized by anything particularly happening in the jail, it may have to do with colleagues or even hearing stories from their colleagues. This may also include stories that they hear from those in their custody. Some stories include difficult things to hear. When you deal with inmates, it can also cause friction on a day to day basis. They may be badgering you, trying to lie to you, or even trick you into doing certain things, all of which can revolve around shame.

Just like anybody else, they sometimes believe that they do not need to help. Reaching out for help is a difficult thing for those in uniform. When they do, you must respond rather quickly. While this is true for substance abuse issues, those in uniform need to have a response within a 24 to 48 hour period or they decide that this is not for them, or worse, they have already acted on their negative thoughts. Their window of interest can close rather quickly, as contemplation of serious negative acts can become all consuming. As a therapist, you must be very responsive and validate their experience. I do not always agree with them, but being able to connect with them is important. I do have an advantage of having worked in this field, so my connection makes it a little easier, although it is a difficult balance.

While it is okay to talk about your past experiences, you cannot talk about it too much or it seems like you are trying to prove something. There is also a view that if you talk too much about your experience, it devalues what they are going through. This second thing applies for all clients. It is also a delicate balance as they are coming to you for a change period. Some of them will not want to talk to you if you seem like a pushover and validate too much. It is an extremely hard balance to create but ultimately, validating while challenging is probably the best balance you will have to connect with them. Direct and to the point is key.

Most of the principles above applied to firefighters/EMTs, as there is also a different type of pressure put on them. It is especially important to realize that being perceived as a hero can be both rewarding and challenging at the same time. Most of the firefighters I work with do not want to be perceived in that way, but the public typically see the firefighter as a 'saving the day' profession versus other types of jobs. I do not want to necessarily debunk that perception, but I also want to encourage everyone to see them as human beings.

It is important to remember that firefighters are human too, as they have long shifts and some in the community settings have perceived them as sleeping all day. They also have a hierarchy that can also be challenging for many. While I I do not want to judge or say that I know better, some of the positions, both in first responders and corrections, have a lot more to do with education and qualifications, rather than experience. As an educated person, I fully understand. But as someone who comes from a blue-collar background, going up the ranks is what I have perceived as more rewarding.

Firefighters work long shifts, and they are not relatively sleeping all the time. While they are not "on high alert", they have a job where they must be ready at any time. They do go to all medical calls. Thanks to their great work in prevention, they deal with a lot less fires as they used to. This may also affect the perception of others, including those who work in the field. With lots of downtime, this can get your mind running and this can also cause mental health concerns. There is also the same type of substance use issues in this field as they are in other law enforcement situations.

Dispatchers in these fields also have a difficult task. While they typically are not ranked necessarily, they have an important job of communicating the information properly to the appropriate first responders group. There could be no calls for a long time, and then suddenly have many calls in a short amount of time. Readiness, as well as ability to transmit the information, is a key stressor that can also come at a cost.

They are typically respected by their colleagues but sometimes, they are treated differently. This could be due to several factors, including telling them they are civilians and not "one of them", as well as being blamed for some of the communication issues. After all, that is their job. This affects how they perceive themselves, including their mental health. I would also add everything else that I have mentioned above for other first responders.

One final note, as I write this chapter, it is June 2020. I know there is a lot of talk of defunding the police. I can understand the principles behind it, as we need to give a chance for police officers to police. Some of the jobs that they do have nothing to do with policing, including working with the homeless, those with mental health issues, substance abuse and things like that. While I think that people in my field can do great work with that population, it is important to remember that the police do much more than that.

Police work can be very fulfilling, but it can also be difficult. One of the things that I feel is misunderstood is that they hear things then most people cannot even conceive. It is an incredibly stressful job and there are certain things that I feel people in my field will not be able to comprehend or deal with properly. Being able to do some of the policing does involve arresting. Maybe not for check fraud, or maybe not for the other stuff that we talked about in the previous paragraph. There are situations, however, where their work must be policing. This includes investigations as well as using their instinct. I also wonder how things such as DUI/DWI will be dealt with. This may also include a court reform issue.

I do not have enough information to explain what policing and law enforcement needs to do on a day-to-day basis. But I do know that it is somewhat different from a therapeutic/counseling position. Learning to work in harmony has happened in different settings, as I have mentioned above. This is where we need to not vilify work by the police but also understand and give them a chance to understand our treatment and how we work. For many years, public health was opposite of public safety and in the last 30 years, this has changed. But it is a difficult change. Learning to balance both needs is difficult at times.

Police have been encouraged to attend mental health first aid (47), and this has been successful for themselves as well as understanding more of our work. Mental health is also discussing various correctional settings for staff to understand how to reach out for help. Stigma about seeking treatment in this field is lessened but still there. As therapists, we need them to understand that mental health treatment is not "reportable" to their departments. This may take some time, but we need to look at how collaboration can be the next step, and not necessarily completely defunding them or doing everything in a treatment modality.

In time, things have changed. Expecting change to be immediate is naive at best. Both sides must work on not vilifying each other, so treatment and policing can work hand in hand and instead of in adversarial ways.

Chapter 9: Trauma and PTSD are NOT the Same

Keywords: Big "T" Trauma, CBT, Defense Mechanisms, EMDR, Guilt, Humanistic, Long Lasting, Neurology, Normalizing, Processing, Shame, Small "t" trauma, Validation

I have enjoyed working with individuals who have trauma issues. Trauma can be hard to discuss, not only for the individuals, but also for the therapist. . Discussing this difficult subject is key to connecting with clients, as they may feel vulnerable. You need to make sure that they know that they will not be judged and that you are able to sit with them while discussing this difficult subject. It is not an easy thing to address or even define. While this chapter will explain my experience in regards to trauma, a more comprehensive outlook is contained by the book: *The Body Keeps the Score* by Bessel Van Der Kolk (48). I highly recommend this book, as many in my field would agree, for a more in depth discussion on trauma.

I work with my clients on this subject more often than I can think of. This is probably due to my other specialties in my work: first responders, correctional staff, and substance use issues. While it is not a universal trait, it happens often in those fields. I do not think I ever went out of my way to become a trauma worker. It did become essential for me to know more about the subject. It is something that I now value in my practice to help me understand some of the underlying issues that may be related to disorders.

I think that defining the term might be the first thing to do. In its simplest form, trauma is a distressing or disturbing experience that an individual has had (49). While trauma can be physical for some, the one I will address here and the one I work heavily on is emotional trauma. At its basis, it is a shock that an individual may have. While going through this shock, the individual experiences difficult experiences in their mind. Some individuals may also define it as stress, but trauma has a longer lasting effect than stress.

It can come in very different forms but it is also important to realize that because of that, trauma is not defined universally. In other words, what is a trauma for one, may not be a trauma for another person. It is not a universal definition but rather a subjective one. For example, if something is traumatic for one person, it does not mean that it is traumatic for another. It can be as simple as the loss of a pet, to the more complex stuff that most people attribute to trauma, like war or unspeakable natural or human occurring events.

It has been discussed as both small "t" trauma versus big "T" trauma (50). Small "t" trauma can be something that is happening right now and that is highly distressing. It does not impact you long-term and does not necessarily involve past traumatic events. It is also defined as emotionally threatening but not necessarily physically threatening. While this is something that has been accepted as a definition in the past, I have decided to agree to disagree with that assessment. I do believe that both can occur. In my experience, trauma can be explained rationally by most human beings. It is a great defense mechanism to not deal with that event. By no means does it necessarily cause PTSD but at times, it can.

Big "T" trauma is more commonly known as post-traumatic stress disorder or PTSD. This can be a life-threatening experience, something that has caused incredibly significant distress that cannot be "shaken off", and includes sexual, physical, and psychological violence. When you think of this type of Trauma, think about experiences that people try to avoid or situations they tried to avoid. They can also lead to poor sleep, unwanted thoughts, self-destructive behavior, or social isolation. Severe anxiety or fear may also occur.

While the common wisdom is to address the Trauma first, it may also be valuable to address the trauma to build a foundation. In other words, being able to look at a trauma and build skills around that can empower a client to talk about the more difficult ones, which include Traumas that may be harder to speak about out loud. I do believe that being able to build the skills necessary to address them is key to moving to the more difficult work regarding that type of trauma.

This usually leads to the bigger discussion of treatment. While treatment can vary from person to person, I generally like to have a situation where we use more of a humanistic approach to discuss the trauma. Letting a person talk about it out loud and being able to not intervene, let's a person's thoughts flow freely on the subject is a great way to let them have that moment. This may help normalize the situation and receive validation from the therapist.

Now, a few words of caution for therapists: it will be tempting to listen to that discussion, try to find solutions, and tell the person to feel better or not to blame themselves for it. While doing this may also be supportive and helpful for the individual, it could also lead to shut down, guilt, and shame. It may also cause the person to feel that they should have found a way to deal with it without seeing a therapist. Most individuals who have traumatic events typically do not reach out after the first traumatic event, but rather after a few occurrences.

The other temptation will be to comfort the individual, with a hug or some form of a professional friendly touch. While touching a client is already a touchy subject on an ethical level, it is probably even harder when someone is talking about their trauma. After all, when someone is telling you something difficult and you try to hug them, they may start thinking about how it affects you, and it may make them stop talking about the trauma. It could also be very triggering for those who have suffered from physical and sexual abuse. Finally, when we hug someone, it tends to stop the individual from talking. Putting words to a traumatic event or events is an important processing time.

There are many treatments for PTSD and trauma, I want to focus on one that I have been doing for a long time which I find helpful and beneficial to clients. Eye Movement Desensitization and Reprocessing (EMDR) (51). This treatment was initiated accidently by Francine Shapiro. Shapiro was on a hike and noticed that she was getting anxious and while she was scanning her environment with her eyes, she felt a relaxation sensation. This led to experiments on a clinical level with eye movement from one side to the other and EMDR was born as a treatment.

EMDR is a highly effective treatment, however the client must be fully cooperative. This treatment can be very exposing, despite what has already been discussed in therapy. Therefore, making sure that the client is completely briefed on what may happen is key to successful treatment (52). It typically involves creating a safe place. A safe place can be somewhere you have been before or that only has fond memories. It can be real or can be imagined. For example, there may be a place that has good memories but may remind you of someone with whom you have negative memories. You can make it a fictitious place by adding or subtracting parts of the scenario. Otherwise, you can create a fictional place that seems right for you. Many individuals choose places they've imagined by reading books or seen in movies.

There is also an author by the name of Laurel Parnell (53) who discussed also having 3 other figures to help the process: the nurturing, protective, and spiritual figure. These are resources that the individual going through treatment can turn to when struggling with parts of the treatment. While these individuals may exist in real life, they do not have to be people who actually exist (just like the safe place). This is especially true for those who have been through trauma and have never had one or any of the three figures discussed above. If a person cannot imagine anyone, it is okay. What I encourage my clients to do is to find people they admire, fictional or real, that exemplifies these figures. By doing so, you increase the resources available to the client. This is essential as the treatment progresses, whether in therapy or outside therapy.

You must make sure the client knows what it is, what it isn't, and how it will progress. You also take a fearless inventory of their history that they do recall. This can be quite difficult for the client. One of the suggestions I make with my clients is to do this type of therapy at the end of the day so that they are not exhausted for their workday or their leisure time. I also discuss the steps that we will be taking, including if it will be used with a visual movement, and auditory movement, or a tactile movement. Clients can choose from a light, to a moving finger, to sound in their ears via a beep, or what they call paddles. Paddles are held in their hands and change sides at a regular beat.

This can usually take 6 to 8 sessions to see progress, or it can take more. This depends on the history of the client as well as the readiness for treatment. As I said before, I like to build a relationship with the client prior to doing this type of treatment, but I have also done this treatment without building a relationship, particularly when it is a referral from a colleague. I also remind clients that they are in control and there is no right way of doing this. The therapist must take a validating and humanistic approach to what is set. Sometimes, you can intervene, but interventions must be kept at a minimum.

As a therapist that likes to talk with my clients and discuss CBT principles, this is very tough for me. I have learned to sit there and listen. One of my clients, one of the first ones to do EMDR, noticed my passivity during this treatment. When I first started doing EMDR 4 years ago, one of my clients told me that it would have been helpful if I had informed them about my change of demeanor. That is why I do it as a disclosure prior to starting EMDR.

I encourage my clients to also look at their grief process in the past, and if there is trauma that is "stuck" in that grief process. This is especially true when people feel that they must be strong when they lose someone that is close to them. While it is important to normalize the reasons they did it, it is also important to validate their feelings and make sure that they probably have to process that grief. It is difficult to accept sometimes but most of my clients, with trust, are willing to do so. Grieving is something that is underestimated and sometimes not done due to outside pressures as well as internal pressures that clients put upon themselves.

I also want to briefly talk about how trauma works in the brain. The theory behind much of trauma is that it has remained in the limbic system and does not reach the cerebral cortex(54). Imagine your brain as a fist. Your arm is your spinal cord, the middle where your fingers turn is the limbic system in the top of your fist is your cerebral cortex. If you look at it that way, signals go from the bottom up. In trauma, it tends to stay stuck in the middle. This is where the fight, flight, or freeze response occurs. This is one of our basic instincts that we have as mammals. With brains that have had Trauma, it tends to be in a fight or flight mode which is perfectly healthy. It is then processed through the cerebral cortex. People with trauma tend to stay in the freeze response and stay stuck in the limbic system, as no neural pathways have been developed to the cerebral cortex in regards to these traumas.

Working with clients to normalize their trauma response is particularly important. Many of my clients felt bad that they did not respond at all. One of my clients also struggled with the fact that her traumatic event felt good at the beginning. There is also lots of shame that goes with not responding to a traumatic event. Therefore it stays stuck in the limbic system. Being able to process it out so speak is important. Letting them know that their response is normal based on their experience makes clients feel "normal".

Trauma is complex even when it is simple. Normalizing, validating, and processing out is the most important part of it. Sometimes it is easier said than done.

Chapter 10:Online Counseling and the Revolution

Keywords: Asynchronous Therapy, Expansion, Losses, New Freudian Couch, Outreach, Pioneer, Text Therapy, Teletherapy, Trauma

When I first heard about teletherapy about 10 years ago, many of my colleagues were skeptic. I frankly was myself. After all, how are we going to be able to look at body language, read affect and things like that? As Lori Gottlieb's colleague had said, it felt like it was therapy with a condom (for the record, I read that quote a few years later) (55).

My first experience with teletherapy happened in a rural area in the state of Vermont. I had taken a job there at the recommendation of a colleague. While I really enjoyed my time in Vermont, there are also very many difficulties in working in a rural area. I grew up in suburbia and I had lived in suburbia most of my life. One of the things that they were attempting to do was to reach individuals who may not have a ride or were unable to attend face-to-face therapy for any type of reasons. I do not want to discuss too much about rural life. but getting from point A to point B without a vehicle can be very daunting.

One of the prescribers was already doing it via telehealth. It was an overly complicated process with a camera that required having proper landlines to protect the privacy and confidentiality of the clients. For those reasons, it was not very popular and was not very practical. I did see, however, progress in those clients and while I did not work with them directly, it certainly raised my interest on the subject. To this day, as far as I know, they continue to do telehealth in even greater numbers and have been widely successful, even being funded by the federal government.

While I did not work with telehealth in Vermont, I was curious and asked lots of questions. I think that is my go-to when I don't know about something. Not pretending I know everything is important to me. The person they gave me who had the most information was someone who tried and was successful at it in another rural part of the state of Maine. He talked about prescriptions mostly and small medical conditions or concerns. I could see the value in that but obviously it won't work for mental health, correct?

I moved back to Massachusetts a year later and did not think much of it. I had some attempts while trying to reach individuals who lived in rural Massachusetts and I had some success, but I felt very handcuffed by the whole process. When you work with individuals who lost their license due to DUIs or DWIs, this may be the only way to reach them. It was okay and I certainly learned to live with it, although I was not a huge fan. I was particularly concerned about missing things in regards to substances and appearance impairment. How could I tell after all?

When I moved to my private practice, I got on a provider online who was HIPAA compliant. It was free and I figured it would be handy to have. I only used it a handful of times in my first year in private practice. When I left the nonprofit world, I had to find ways to make this part-time private practice a full-time practice. This was one of the ways that I could do it. While it was not widely used and even the clients were very skeptical, I had used it with mild success when people cannot make their appointments.

I continue to be concerned about missing certain cues, especially if it is physical, or even if they were fidgeting or anything else like that. Could I tell if they were nervous if I could not see their torso or body overall? When they were looking away, were they doing it because of avoidance, or something else? After all distraction does occur in this type of setting. I did not use it a lot but I certainly wanted to give it a try.

I then started working with an online company that did asynchronous text, voice, and video on a secure with network. Asynchronous meant that they can text and leave a voice message any time and I would respond twice a day. So it was not direct text. It could be an exchange of direct text if you arranged it that way but ultimately, it was typically delayed. There was also a video option to do live video sessions, but it was not popular at the time. I was originally hoping for more my video but it did not occur as much as I wish.

This company reached out to me via LinkedIn and I interviewed. It seemed to be a very rigorous process at the time, but in hindsight, it was not. It did prepare me for some of the stuff that would need to be done on a text level service. While this was a start-up company, they also wanted to make sure that we had retention so that the financial payments would continue to come in. I was less of a fan of that. I do have to admit that they were originally very eager to have successful therapists on the platform and were supportive of therapists when it first started. I wanted to connect with clients and see if text therapy as well as video therapy could work in the long term. It was also a revenue that I needed in my private practice.

In the first year, I saw quick results. There were not many regulations at the time, so I was seeing people from different states as well as different countries across the world. By the end of year one, I had reached clients on every continent except Antarctica, I had worked with individuals in eight provinces in Canada, as well as the 50 states in the United States. I saw where it could work and I certainly became much more attuned to that work.

Where did it work? It really worked with individuals who travel a lot and would like to be in therapy, but are typically unable to meet face-to-face. They were able to get a therapist that would be responding to them in an asynchronous way through text. You could also leave voice messages and the response was asynchronous also. It felt very convenient for them and they were happy about the treatment.

I also found that people were able to get services in very remote areas. In some areas in the United States and Canada, there might only be a few therapists for a 100 mile radius. I ended up connecting with individuals who are unable to connect to therapists in their area. For lack of availability or just simply not connecting with anyone in that area, it was helpful to them to have that space to talk about anything they wanted at any given time of the day. They knew how it worked and they were happy to get responses the way they were received.

I also found that individuals were able to write or talk out loud about things that they may have not shared with anyone else. There was something about seeing someone's eyes that was difficult for some, particularly trauma. I had several clients who would write in great detail about traumas that they had had in their lives that they were unable to speak about. It was very striking when a few clients even wrote: "I would've never been able to say this with you in the same room looking at me". In my opinion, this was the new Freudian couch.

When you think about it, the Freudian couch was helpful because you did not have the "judgmental look" of the therapist. They were able to open up by looking at a blank wall and not have to look anyone in the eye. Psychoanalytic treatment opened many people to therapy and lots of their past traumas and issues were uncovered by having that space. And therapy was more than once a week. I can feel the parallels with this type of counseling.

I continued to have many skeptical colleagues. Many of them were not willing to try it and had called it a fad. They also do not want to try video sessions, as this was not very telling about where the client was at. In other words, it was believed by some of my colleagues that clients would not want to make the effort to attend. I found it particularly interesting that most of them discounted it without even trying. I wondered sometimes if it was intimidation, or simply unable to look at it in a different way. I will never judge my colleagues, as this was their choice and that is okay.

In time, more video sessions occurred and I was able to find a great flow with this type of treatment. I highly recommend it for those who feel that text, voice, video therapy would be beneficial to them. I am also very realistic because I do not believe that this is for everyone. Some clients try it and feel too distracted. Others don't like the lack of human contact. As you have heard me say many times, you must meet the client where they're at and some clients cannot do this, which is okay and other clients thrive on this service.

As of this writing in June 2020, there is a pandemic going on. All my colleagues went to telehealth in the last four months. The groups that I belong to on Facebook who are always anti-teletherapy have suddenly become huge fans and some of them do not even want to go back to their offices. I find it interesting that until they were forced to try, they had prejudice about it. Now that they have tried it, it seems revolutionary. I continue to work with telehealth companies, as well as my own HIPAA compliant platform. I will never stop using teletherapy for those who feel this would be helpful.

Many people have embraced telehealth and I am happy for this development. I do feel like a pioneer but ultimately, many others have done it before me. With time, this type of therapy will only become more common in my opinion.

Chapter 11:Expression Use To Help Treatment

Keywords: Accusation, Anger, Arrogance, CBT, Common Sense, Control, Decision Making, Family, Hate, Indifference, Interpretation, Love, Privacy, Secrecy, Trust

Just like every therapist, I have some expressions that I use on a regular basis. We can talk about different techniques, whether it's CBT, behavioral, EMDR, psychoanalytic, Gestalt, and many others that I'm forgetting, but I feel the words you use become part of your therapy in a much bigger fashion than the actual techniques that you use.

I named my private practice "Straight to the Point Therapy". I need to thank my colleague and friend, the late Starr Beauvais, who also is in my lineage for Reiki treatment, for coming up with that name. It is something that I do in my day-to-day life and frankly, in my treatment style. I am honest without being untactful. I also believe that honesty is what makes people grow and with the population I work with, very essential to create a bond. Many of my clients have said that my private practice name is really a representation of who I am with them. I think that is a huge compliment.

While I don't want to go into it too much, I think it comes from growing up in Québec and having the family that I had. But my parents were very direct and my immediate first-degree family, which I saw every week, were direct with each other and I learned from that. I think it also created better communication in the long-term. This can, of course, cause some issues, but learning to translate it with thoughtfulness and tact is part of what I have done in my private practice. I can thank my family for this skill.

I also think that this since English is my second language, I struggle with some of the "bigger words". Being able to use more direct and simpler words has created a bond with most of my clients. It is of course, not for everyone. But I do believe that I have the right clientele, and most people who match with me look for that type of treatment. I have found that many of my clients do not care for flowery words or intense validation but rather direct statements and concrete ideas.

I am going to just write the expressions I use and can tell you the context.

Are you willing to be hated to be loved? (Es-tu prêt de te faire haïr pour te faire aimer).

Funny thing, this comes from the misheard lyric in a song by Eric Lapointe, "Fais Un Bum de Toé"(56). The actual lyric is: "Es-tu capable de t'haïr pour t'faire aimer?". But the one I use makes more sense in a therapeutic way. There are a lot of people who are not willing to speak their mind because they are afraid of not being loved for what they say. Learning to be able to accept that people may not like you in a moment or even hate you can frankly, lead to great things. It goes hand-in-hand with another expression that I use which is "the opposite of love is not hate, it's indifference". Learning that you cannot hate someone you do not know or feel you know is a particularly important part of treatment. Hate comes from loving someone in the past, and hate typically does not last forever. I can go on about how hate is hardened anger but that is a discussion for another time.

It is what you make of it

This comes from another expression that I've heard before which is: "it is what it is". One of my former colleagues used to use that one a lot. I think that it does not really capture everything. Things are the way you interpret them and are not necessarily what they are. After all, a spilled soda is just a spilled soda unless you interpret it differently. What is said to you, when you just look at the words, can be quite simple. Our interpretation plays a factor. This reminds my clients that interpretation plays a huge factor in their own lives, coming from my background in cognitive behavioral therapy. Learning to see how we interpret things can help us understand our biases.

Pink elephant in the room

I like to use this one when individuals do not want to truly express what they are feeling. This is especially helpful when clients tiptoe around the subject that may be difficult. I typically name the pink elephant in the room. I also use another example that is similar in regards to avoidance. I tell my clients that they do not have to worry, but there is a stuffed parakeet behind them that I just got. I tell them not to worry about it, it is just there, I don't think it will bother them, but I just wanted to let them know. My typical next question is what can you think about right now, which inevitably comes to the parakeet. This reminds individuals not to avoid things, but instead to name them. (For the record, I don't have a stuffed parakeet.)

Communication versus accusation

This comes from my experience with anger management, as well as couples counseling. When we use 'I' sentences, it typically means that we are communicating how we feel. When you use the word "you", it appears to be much more accusatory. Learning to be able to communicate things versus accusing people can help how interactions can go. It is difficult to work with accusations, as people tend to react very negatively to those. Even if they are true. Even if you love the other person. People cannot change how you feel, however communicating with I statements can become quite a savior.

Saying no is the hardest thing to do

People struggle with saying no. This is probably people pleasing, but I also think that we learn, through social settings, whether it is school or work, that saying no means you are rejecting something. They could also be interpreted as negative. After all, "no" is not exactly positive. But then, I talk about how saying no for yourself is beneficial and positive. When you prioritize pleasing others or pushing yourself to a limit that may break you, this can only hurt you. Saying no will be the best gift for yourself as well as for others.

The one thing you control is your response

One of the things that happens is that people want to control others with what they say. "If I say that, they won't be able to say anything but _____". I remind individuals that this usually does not work out for anyone. When we are upset, and we feel like we need to control either the situation or the other person, it typically leads to even more frustration and difficulties. By knowing that you can control yourself, it makes it easier. Learning to control your own thoughts around things through pauses as well as neural plasticity can be the greatest thing that can happen to you.

Common sense is not that common

Too many times, we expect that people will do the right thing or that they know what logically should come next. While this could happen on a regular basis, sometimes it does not. I typically hear from my clients that common sense would dictate _____ but if you look at things based on emotions, as well as situation and how people think, common sense is not that common. After all, not everyone thinks the same way you do.

Insanity is doing the same thing repeatedly expecting a different result

This expression is typically credited to Albert Einstein. If you research the Internet, it states that there is no clear indication that he said that(57). There have been many different findings on the origin of this statement so I will not credit one person, but I certainly won't credit myself. I usually talk about this one when my clients keep on doing the same thing hoping that situations or people will change. Obviously they don't. And learning to deal with it in a different way usually turns out to be much more efficient.

Your thoughts are not who you are

This comes from many research that suggests that humans have anywhere from 12,000 to 60,000 thoughts in a day (58). Our thoughts are not typically who we are but they are there. I usually accompany this statement with this fact and then discuss how it is important to remember which thoughts we hold onto, and which one will continue to have a grasp on. It then leads to more questions about why we hold on to that thought and what does that mean, whether it is historical, situational or about a person.

Your feelings are valid but may not be right

Never devalue anyone's feelings. We can feel whatever we want. This is important to remember, not only for therapists, but also for ourselves. It is important to realize that individuals feel different things. It is quite a challenge to tell someone that they may not be right. This can shock someone but also can lead to a shift in their thought process about how things are. We may feel a certain way about different things but is it right? Are we feeling that because of our past or something else?

There is a difference between privacy and secrecy

I attribute this statement from an iTunes original by Alanis Morrissette (59). We can respect a person's privacy, as they have every right to keep things about themselves private. But when it is secret, it involves shame, fear, and, at times, trauma. We cannot keep secrets from ourselves and we need to be transparent by being truthful to ourselves. Being able to be truthful to your therapist is a particularly good thing. When you hear the secret out loud it may not be as bad as you think. I also believe that secrecy keeps us in a cage. Having this discussion can be extremely helpful around trauma and difficulties in the past.

Trust is a tricky thing: it is hard to get and easy to lose

When I help my clients realize that trust is a difficult thing, I use this as an opportunity to help individuals who struggle with trusting someone else. I also remind them that it is difficult for others to trust them if the trust has been broken in the past. It ultimately leads to a conversation about trusting yourself and doing the right thing, and not necessarily counting on others to trust them. I have also been known to discuss this particularly in those who have struggled with substance use disorders. Once you do the right thing for yourself, others will start noticing it and trust can be slowly won back.

Perfection leads to arrogance

Many of my clients tend to be perfectionists. Perhaps it is related to anxiety and depression, perhaps it is related to trauma, and I tend to see it for those with substance use issues. Once my client talks about the perfection they want to achieve, I remind them that the perfect person has an issue which is arrogance. Therefore they are not perfect. While this is said in a way that makes the client laugh, I use this opportunity and opening to discuss more realistic goals. I also discuss that high achieving is okay but perfection is the problem.

The story I am telling myself

This comes from one of my favorite authors, Brené Brown (60). I could probably write an entire chapter on what Brené talks about and how vulnerability is the most courageous thing you will ever do. I like to use this statement in couples counseling as well as those who are having difficulties in their relationships. When someone makes you upset or your emotions start taking over, own up to what you are saying to yourself about what is going on. No one can take that away from you and it can lead to a great discussion, especially if they are able to also do the same thing and use the same statement.

Not making a decision is making a decision

This was told to me by a supervisor many years ago and I truly continue to use it on a regular basis. I have many clients who get stuck in a dilemma and do not decide about it for weeks or even months. After a while, I use the sentence above to make them realize that there has been a decision, but they do not want to see it. They absolutely appreciate it. Then they start looking at what they want to decide.

Chapter 12: Demystifying Therapy

Keywords: Assumption, Availability, Boundaries, Change, Complex, Curiosity, Defining, Empathy, Fixing, Flexibility, Openness, Reliability, Self-Care, Schema, Silence, Tools, Vulnerability

As I said in my introduction, I remember when I started out as a therapist, I thought that I would just plop myself down and listen to what a person was saying and move on to the next client. I quickly learned that relationships with clients are complex and I need to nurture my relationship with them, as well as myself.

It is human nature to make assumptions. We have created schemas (schemata). A schema represents knowledge about concepts to simplify our access to it in our brain. To predict the world as a therapist, we tend to see patterns in other people's behavior that we have seen before. This is a helpful tool, but we also need to realize that we do not know that person's story, and continuing to be curious is essential to the long-term health of the therapist. If we are not curious, we will push many clients away.

This is where empathy comes to play. Learning to put yourself in someone else's shoes is important for therapists. It is also something that we need to teach while we work with clients. I also think that empathy can lead to a closer bond with the client. Clients who come to therapy may have trust issues, or struggle with different things, and you need to make sure that they believe that you will listen to them. It is also a way to make them feel that you will be there for them. Reliability of the therapist is paramount to the therapeutic relationship.

By no means does this mean that you must always be available to the clients you serve. I am sure that some people will be surprised to read this but let me explain: if you are always available, it will reduce the effectiveness of the client. Clients who rely too much on therapists are very problematic, as the client will not learn how to solve the problems for themselves, the therapist will feel stretched out, and a less than therapeutic bond will be created. You can support your client in their time of need, as I have done multiple times, but you also must have boundaries.

This is another Brené Brown concept. Boundaries are "simply our lists of what's okay and what's not okay" (61). In other words, what you feel is acceptable versus what is not acceptable. Being clear about those boundaries is important and defining them at the beginning of any session with a client will take you a long way. Boundaries are not only for the therapist but also for the client: the client will know where you stand, and you will be able to set those limits as needed. I also like her words on how to explain, which is "clear is kind, unclear is unkind" (62).

One last thing about boundaries, they can be porous, rigid, or flexible. When they are rigid, it leads to frustration on both parties. If you make them porous, it will be broken on a regular basis and limits will not be set. Learning to be flexible is key. This is probably good advice for therapy. Your flexibility will be important throughout your sessions, which will show authenticity on your part.

Being able to tell your clients that you are not perfect is a good start. I like to also remind my clients, as I have said before, that I am bad with names. Therefore, in addition to boundaries, I also talk about things in which I struggle. This shows openness to your client which is also important. Obviously, the session is about the client and not about you. Some therapists start talking about their problems and do not listen to their clients anymore. There have been many clients who have reported that frustration with me in the past.

Another thing that I like to tell therapists to avoid is feeling pity for the client. While clients have had very tough lives, feeling bad for them may make the relationships less than therapeutic. Clients may hesitate to talk about things because of that, and you want them to be able to talk about things and not think about your own feelings as a therapist, but rather their own. I also cautioned many therapists to say that they know how the client feels: that is Psychology 101. I think sometimes, with too much training, we tend to forget.

In the beginning of my career, one of my colleagues had reminded me that you need to be able to define the word. This being a second language for me, that came very easily but let me explain what I mean by that. Let us use, for example, the word anger. Because I have done anger management in my career, one of the first things I do when individuals struggle with anger, is I ask them to define it. After all, not everyone has the definition from the dictionary or from Google. By defining it, you can see the interpretation the client has about that word and how to work with that.

This comes back to meeting the client where they are at in life. If you do not show curiosity in regards to their life and how to interpret certain things, you will also forget important things, such as their self-identity, whether it is socioeconomic, sexual orientation, race, gender, and other things like that. This will lead clients to not feel validated or understood, which, in turn, will probably lead to clients not coming in therapy or not finding it helpful, eventually leading them to confirm their bias that therapy never works.

I have heard many times that therapy does not work for certain clients. I always respect that point of view because of the points made above, but I also understand a few other things that may lead to that point of view. The first thing is that vulnerability is not a given. Some clients may be resistant because of their past, how they grew up, and other factors like that. It is important to make sure to not take it for granted. I usually start talking about how therapy works with clients who are more resistant. I can remind them of how they will be supported, but also that a therapist does not actually do the changing, they do.

Therapists tend to offer tools for people to work on themselves or for the changes that they want. I remind myself of this all the time when I feel that I am not as helpful as I wish. While it is important to be self-critical and look at our work, we also need to remind ourselves that the work must be done by the client and not by the therapist. I also like to remind myself that change takes at least six months to be remarkably effective (63). I know the common knowledge is that change takes 21 days, but the actual statement is change takes *at least* 21 days (64).

I love the common wisdom, but I also know that changing our thought process is difficult, specifically for those who have held those beliefs for a long time. Being supportive by exploring the individual strengths versus their weaknesses can be helpful. I come back to the wisdom that I once heard from, of all things, professional wrestling. It stated that if they emphasize their strengths and work on their weaknesses, they will tend to be better professionals (I am paraphrasing). Be curious on how they feel about themselves in general, but particularly on their strengths and weaknesses so you can support them better.

Many of my clients have also benefited from a conversation regarding if what is happening in their lives is due to a situation versus who they are as people. In other words, there are situations that are just difficult and not necessarily a reflection on who they are. As my clients would confirm, I sometimes remind them that a situation can just suck and has nothing to do with them. The changes that they want to do on themselves is important but if it is a situational thing, we have to note our control in regard to the situation, as well as if there's things that can be done around that.

This also comes back to the client making the change, not the therapist. One of my favorite things is to have a client talk out loud about their problem in using some of the techniques we have spoken about in the past. I have enjoyed being in situations where my clients realize that they are doing it and in a funny way, make faces or state that we have already talked about that. I will save the words they sometimes use but I promise that the words they use can be profane, but they are meant in a goodhearted way.

It is also important sometimes to not talk. When a client is struggling with something and does not speak for a short while, therapists tend to want to fill that void. Resisting to fill that void will push the client to speak. After all, no one likes that "dead air" right? I think this forces exploration by the client, and it has been used by many therapists in the past. Silence is golden as the saying goes.

I also, at times, use the "Columbo Technique". Columbo was a TV detective who sometimes used the information a person offered him that was contradictory. In other words, he will let someone talk and then say something like "I'm confused. You said _____ earlier but now you are saying _____. Can you help me understand this contradictory information?". By being curious and really paying attention, it is sometimes useful to use information provided and show how they are sometimes contradictory. This technique is useful to see how the client will solve their cognitive dissonance.

One final note: therapists are incredibly good at talking about self-care, but they are incredibly poor at doing it for themselves. This is especially true for newer therapists. As you grow in the profession, you learn how to take care of yourself and do things that you enjoy. At the beginning of their careers, there is always an idealization of their work and how they will fix things. I have never "fixed" a client in all my life. I tend to struggle to fix myself but with good self-care, I get better at doing that.

Self-care is sometimes misunderstood. I think self-care has a lot to do with doing things for yourself that you are not obligated to do. I always hear people telling me that they will get their hair or nails done, but I think that that is maintenance in my opinion. Self-care has a lot to do with doing things you enjoy which may not be enjoyable for others. I also tend to look for self-care activities that a person can do themselves, as this also makes them concentrate on them and almost makes it a mindfulness exercise.

Doing therapy both for the client and the therapist is not magical. There are no mirrors or tricks, it is a process that involves efforts that can be fruitful when done in the proper way. What is the proper way? Depends on the client, depends on a therapist.

Conclusion

While therapy can be very daunting, it can also be a very eye-opening situation for yourself. You need to give it time as well to realize that the process does not happen overnight. Change can take at least six months and when you discover these changes, it sometimes leads to more discoveries that need to be discussed. I do really believe that having the different skills and outlooks as described in this book can be beneficial. But by no means do I believe that this is the only way to do so.

Many of my clients have given me nicknames. Here are some that I remember. One of my favorites is being called "Buddha" by one of my clients. I never asked if it was about what I look like or the wisdom I discuss. When you know more about practicing Buddhism, it states that we are all Buddhas so I will take it.

Other clients have said to me that I make their brain itch. When I asked what that meant, they told me that I used logic and cognitive skills for them to think about the problem in a different light. This also led to lots of reflecting and thinking about other people's behaviors as well as their own. I think that making someone's brain itch is probably one of the best compliments you can get as a therapist, as this is the goal of our work.

My clients have also thrown out the traditional swear words at me that George Carlin made famous. While I know some of my colleagues may see that as a lack of respect or as something negative, I do not perceive it the same way. The clients that have said that to me, for the most part because we had gone through some cognitive restructuring and when the next session or so comes around, they go back to old thought processes. I then use their own logic to bring them back to the same conclusion. This is typically when I get sworn at, a sign of respect that I receive from them as human beings.

Other clients have sworn at my signs in my office, as they do not like the sayings on it. Not because they are not good, but that they are reminders of how to think differently. I have talked about some of my expressions, as well as other signs. Ultimately, realizing that we can use some of the small expressions to rewire their brain makes me feel like it can be beneficial.

Every client is different and every therapist is different. My style has fit me since day one. While I give myself permission to change at any time, as change occurs frequently, I felt that this has been the most authentic that I can be. Hopefully, it leads to more authenticity from the clients that I see.

References

1. Burns, David D. (1981) Feeling Good: The New Mood Therapy. Penguin Books, 1981

2. https://data.bls.gov/projections/occupationProj

3.https://www.thesun.co.uk/news/4995314/david-cassidy-death-last-words-daughter/

4.Frieswyk, S. & al. (1986) Therapeutic alliance: Its place as a process and outcome variable in dynamic psychotherapy research. Journal of Consulting and Clinical Psychology, Vol 54(1), Feb 1986, 32-38

5.https://www.bustle.com/articles/78842-women-take-7-selfies-before-posting-one-spend-5-hours-a-week-taking-photos-of#:~:text=A%20study%20conducted%20by%20Feel Unique,seven%20selfies%20before%20posting%20o ne.&text=FeelUnique%2C%20the%20beauty%20site %20that,to%20two%20social%20media%20sites.

6.https://www.verywellmind.com/who-can-provide-psychotherapy-2795763

7.https://www.theglobeandmail.com/news/national/qu ebec-chanteuse-alys-robi-triumphed-over-adversity/article581790/

8.https://genius.com/George-carlin-the-seven-words-you-can-never-say-on-television-annotated

9.https://www.imdb.com/title/tt0701117/characters/nm0144657

10.Freud, S. (1925) "Die Verneinung"

11.Festinger, L. (1962) Cognitive dissonance. Scientific American. 207 (4): 93–10

12.Rogers, C. (1951) Client-centered Therapy: Its Current Practice, Implications and Theory. Houghton Mifflin

13.https://www.quora.com/How-big-is-Howard-Stern-s-radio-audience-on-Sirius

14.De Larochellière, L (1990)Cash City Produced by Luc De Larochellière, Joe Petrella & Marc Pérusse. Album:Sauvez mon âme

15.https://themanifest.com/social-media/how-people-use-social-media-2018

16.https://www.helpguide.org/articles/mental-health/social-media-and-mental-health.htm

17.https://www.youtube.com/watch?v=XXhk448-GAQ

18.https://www.asam.org/Quality-Science/definition-of-addiction

19. Norcross J. (2002), Psychotherapy relationships that work. Oxford University Press

20.https://www.empathia.com/the-magic-of-21-days/#:~:text=It%20turns%20out%20the%2021,wrote%20Psycho%2DCybernetics%20in%201960.

21. Tiemens, Bea & al. (2019), Lower versus higher frequency of sessions in starting outpatient mental health care and the risk of a chronic course; a naturalistic cohort study, BMC Psychiatry.

22.https://www.sciencedirect.com/topics/neuroscience/neuropsychology#:~:text=Developmental%20neuropsychology%20is%20intricately%20involved,any%20given%20point%20in%20time.

23.https://courses.lumenlearning.com/wmopen-psychology/chapter/outcome-parts-of-the-brain/

24.https://www.neuroscientificallychallenged.com/blog/know-your-brain-midbrain

25. Kandel, Eric (2000). Principles of Neural Science. McGraw-Hill.

26.https://psychotherapy-center.com/therapy-methods/remap/introducing-quick-remap/a-tale-of-two-brains-how-remap-can-help/

27.Shapiro, F. (2018). Eye movement desensitization and reprocessing (EMDR) therapy: Basic principles, protocols, and procedures (3rd ed.). Guilford Press

28.Chamberlin, D. E. (2019). The predictive processing model of EMDR. Frontiers in Psychology, 10, Article 2267

29.https://drarielleschwartz.com/how-does-emdr-therapy-work-dr-arielle-schwartz/#.X0LmrMhKiso

30. Hase, m. et al. (2015) Eye movement desensitization and reprocessing (EMDR) therapy in

the treatment of depression: a matched pairs study in an inpatient setting. Brain Behavior 5(6)

31.Hase, M & al. (2015) Eye movement desensitization and reprocessing (EMDR) therapy in the treatment of depression: a matched pairs study in an inpatient setting. Brain Behavior 5(6)

32.National Science Foundation (2005)

33.Sarno, John E.(1991) Healing Back Pain: The Mind-Body Connection, Grand Central Publishing

34.Margets, Edward L (1950) History of the Word Psychosomatic, Can Med Assoc J., 402-404

35.https://healthblog.uofmhealth.org/wellness-prevention/can-an-elimination-diet-help-you-lose-weight

36.Brogan, Kelly (2016) A Mind of Her Own, Harper Thorsons

37.Rosenhahn, B. & al. (2007) Human Motion - Understanding, Modelling, Capture and Animation. Volume 36 in *Computational Imaging and Vision*, Springer

38.https://www.brainfitacademy.com/

39.Pease, B & Pease, A (2006)The Definitive Book of Body Language: The Hidden Meaning Behind People's Gestures and Expressions, Bantam

40.Ekman, P. (2007) Emotions Revealed, Second Edition: Recognizing Faces and Feelings to Improve

Communication and Emotional Life, Weidenfeld & Nicolson

41.Prebish, Charles (2019) Is Buddhism a Religion? Lion's Roar Magazine

42.Surya Das, Lama (1998) Awakening The Buddha Within, Harmony

43.NIDA (2010) Comorbidity: Addiction and Other Mental Illnesses Research Report

44.NIDA (2003) Diagnosis and Treatment of Drug Abuse in Family Practice - American Family Physician Monograph. *National Institute on Drug Abuse*

45.Brand, R. (2017) Recover: Freedom From Our Addictions, Picador

46.Bledsoe, B (2003) Critical incident stress management (CISM): benefit or risk for emergency services?, Prehosp Emerg Care, April-May (2): 272-279

47.https://www.mentalhealthfirstaid.org/

48.Van der Kolk, B (2015) The Body Keeps the Score: Brain, Mind, and Body in the Healing of Trauma, Penguin Books

49.https://integratedlistening.com/

50.https://www.goodtherapy.org/blog/big-t-and-little-t-trauma-and-how-your-body-reacts-to-it-1019154

51.Shapiro, F. (2018). Eye movement desensitization and reprocessing (EMDR) therapy: Basic principles, protocols, and procedures (3rd ed.). Guilford Press

52.Shapiro, F. (2018). Eye movement desensitization and reprocessing (EMDR) therapy: Basic principles, protocols, and procedures (3rd ed.). Guilford Press

53.Parnell, L. (2008) Tapping In: A Step-by-Step Guide to Activating Your Healing Resources Through Bilateral Stimulation, Amazon.com Services LLC

54.Fenster, R.& al. (2018) Brain circuit dysfunction in post-traumatic stress disorder: from mouse to man. Nat Rev Neurosci. 2018 Sep; 19(9): 535–551

55.Gottlieb, L. (2019) Maybe You Should Talk With Someone. Houghton Mifflin Harcourt

56.Lapointe, E. (2004) Fais un bum de toé. Produced by Stéphane Dufour. Album Coupable

57.https://quoteinvestigator.com/2017/03/23/same/

58.National Science Foundation (2005)

59.Morrisette, A. (2004) Itunes Original

60.Brown, B. (2015) Rising Strong: How the Ability to Reset Transforms the Way We Live, Love, Parent, and Lead. Random House

61.Brown, B. (2017) Braving the Wilderness: The Quest for True Belonging and the Courage to Stand Alone. Random House

62.Brown, B. (2018) Dare to Lead: Brave Work. Tough Conversations. Whole Hearts. Random House

63.Vallis, M (2013) Counselling—How Do I Know If I Am Doing It Well? The Development of the Behaviour Change Counselling Scale, Canadian Journal of Diabetes, 37(1), 18-36
64.https://www.empathia.com/the-magic-of-21-days/#:~:text=It%20turns%20out%20the%2021,wrote%20Psycho%2DCybernetics%20in%201960.

Acknowledgements

This book would not have been possible without many contributing factors. I want to first thank my clients and colleagues who have encouraged me to write a book about my style of therapy. It has been mentioned to me throughout the years and you made this possible.

Thank you to my editor, Ashley Furtado. Your patience and understanding were truly appreciated. You adapted to my style of writing in a very graceful and understanding way. I am eternally grateful. And thank you Mike Gleason for making this connection possible.

Thanks, Brendon LeBlanc, for the cover art and for truly understanding my vision and making it happen. Our friendship for over 20 years may have contributed to the success also.

Thank you to my beta readers, David Bassano, Jay Ball, Doreen Bove, and Serena Neslusan. Your feedback was imperative for the success of this book.

Thanks to my Mom, Nicole Bisson, for being present in my life, despite the distance that separates us for the past 21 years.

Thanks to my Dad, Peter Bisson, for always supporting me and making sure I do everything I do with passion. I miss you and you are still in my thoughts. Rest in peace.

Thank you to my best friends, Jocelyn Houle, Francesco Pensato, and Hélène Dupuis for being there for me for 30+years. You mean a lot to me.

Most importantly, thank you to my girls, Catherine and Christina. They have always inspired me to push myself and also have been patient through this process of creating and editing. I love you.

About Steve Bisson

Born and raised in Montréal, Québec, Canada, Steve Bisson moved to Massachusetts in 1999 after completing is Bachelors at McGill University to pursue his dream of working in the mental health field.

He has been a therapist for 17 years and has owned his private practice, Straight to the Point Therapy, since 2011. Steve has been using telehealth services since 2015. Trained in Cognitive Behavioral Therapy at Assumption College for his Masters, Steve has worked in diverse fields, including community outpatient teams, the criminal justice field, as a member of a mental health crisis team, as well as a trainer for first responders and correctional staff on mental health and substance abuse.

EMDR trained, he has processed trauma and bereavement issues throughout his career. When not working, Steve enjoys being outdoors and spending time with his two daughters and two cats.

Connect with Steve Bisson

Follow me on Instagram:
https://www.instagram.com/stevebissonlmhc/

Follow me on Facebook:
https://www.facebook.com/SteveBissonLMHC

My website: http://stevebissonlmhc.com/

My Instagram for this book:
https://www.instagram.com/findingyourwaythroughtherapy/

Made in the USA
Middletown, DE
04 November 2020

23338847R00096